I hope you enjoy!

Always Forward #→

PRAISE FOR
HEAR THESE TRUTHS

"Clark has written a no-nonsense leadership book that we need now more than ever. The one that makes you look in the mirror and ask, 'are my actions that of a leader of others or are they only self-serving?'"

— Drew Ward
Corporate Executive Chef,
Artisanal Brewing Ventures

"In today's world, Clark brings straightforward guidance about becoming a better leader."

— Nicholas Hutchison
Founder of BookThinkers

"Providing out-of-the-box lessons, Clark's book sets the new standard by providing the hard truths on leadership."

— Timothy Martin
Chief Strategy Officer

PRAISE FOR
HEAR THESE TRUTHS

"An honest take on the not-so-glamourous but essential side of leadership."

— Jenna Carlton
Content Creator, "The Millennial Veteran"

"The truths in this book are exactly that... simple truths. But so often, we forget the simplest things in life. We forget to incorporate ourselves into our leadership styles. We forget to listen to others. We forget that others can't read our thoughts. We get busy... and we forget. This book is there to be a constant reminder for us not to forget the most important things when it comes to leadership. And if our job as leaders is to create more leaders, then we definitely can't forget the truth. Thank you Jeff Clark for creating such a simple way to remind us all."

— Tracy Borreson
Branding Consultant & Leadership Coach

PRAISE FOR
HEAR THESE TRUTHS

"Clark says it how it is, no candy coating, but still applicable to anyone in a leadership role. This is a must-read."

— Mike Patredis
Head Golf Coach, Eaton High School

"Clark brings a much-needed visionary plan for speaking guidance on becoming a leader others want to follow."

— Carl Shawn Watkins
*Army Veteran and CEO of
Carl Shawn Watkins Consulting*

"Jeff has undoubtedly put together the hard truths of leadership and how to use them. A must-read for leaders in any field!"

— Chrissy McDaniel
*NRP, EMS Operations Manager
& State Recruiter*

HEAR THESE TRUTHS

THE ULTIMATE GUIDE TO BUILDING YOUR LEADERSHIP ALGORITHM

JEFF CLARK

Hear These Truths:
The Ultimate Guide to Building Your Leadership Algorithm

Copyright © 2022 by Jeff Clark

All rights reserved. No part of this publication may be reproduced, distributed, or transmitted in any form or by any means (including photocopying, recording, or other electronic or mechanical methods), without the prior written permission of the publisher, except in the case of brief quotations in a book review and certain other noncommercial uses permitted by copyright law.

First Edition

Due to the dynamic nature of the internet, web addresses or links contained in this publication may have changed since publication and may no longer be valid. Any links which are included in this publication are provided as a convenience and for informational purposes only; they do not constitute an endorsement or an approval by the publisher. Tactical 16 Publishing, as well as its employees and/or affiliates, bears no responsibility for the accuracy, legality or content of the content on third-party websites.

Published by Tactical 16 Publishing
Colorado Springs, Colorado
www.Tactical16.com

ISBN: 978-1-943226-65-8 (paperback)

CONTENTS

Foreword v
Preparation 1
Algorithms 9
Power of Purpose 17
Part 1: Effort 25
    Chapter 1: Leadership 27
    Chapter 2: Self-Licking Ice Cream Cone 33
    Chapter 3: Empowerment and Confidence 39
    Chapter 4: Decisions 45
    Chapter 5: False Ideas 51
    Chapter 6: Y.O.U. – Your Own Understanding 59
    Chapter 7: Values 65
Part II: Process 77
    Chapter 8: Daily Habits 81
    Chapter 9: Deliberate Development 87
    Chapter 10: Plus, Minus, Equal 95
    Chapter 11: Coaching and Mentoring 101
    Chapter 12: Change 107
    Chapter 13: The 30–60–90 Rule 113
    Chapter 14: Strategy 121
    Chapter 15: Communication, Part 1 127
    Chapter 16: Communication, Part 2 133
Part III: Progress 141
    Chapter 17: AAR – Active Listening, Accountability, and Responsibility 145
    Chapter 18: Performance 153
    Chapter 19: Vulnerability 159

Chapter 20: Flexibility 165
Chapter 21: Innovate and Motivate 171
Chapter 22: Culture and Dynamics 183
Chapter 23: Failure 189
Chapter 24: Leadership is Not for Sale 193
Chapter 25: Final Message 199
Acknowledgments 203
About the Author
About the Publisher

FOREWORD

I've been working professionally for over nineteen years, working in various organizations, as well as being a father and a husband. My life is blessed with four healthy and smart kids, who I no doubt believe will do great things. I couldn't be luckier.

I spent over fifteen years with the US government, twelve of them on active duty with the Air Force, and another three as an employed civilian. Uncle Sam has been good to me. My years in the Air Force are some of my best memories, made with the most incredible people. I'll forever be thankful for my time in the military, and I bleed Air Force blue.

I have plenty of friends and connections in the other services, with a deep respect for their service and mission. My family has a rich history of military service, from my oldest son to my grandfather dating back to World War II.

Military experience molded who I am. My time influenced my leadership philosophy, ideas, and concepts shared in these pages while serving. I grew as a follower, as a leader, and as a professional. The Air Force did not recognize me as the 2019 Air Force Civilian Supervisor of the Year (Installation category, A1) because I did the same things in 2019 that I did at the start of my career. Recognition of that level came because I grew as time went on. I had successes and failures, obtained new tricks and trades, and most importantly, I learned to learn.

Like many other veterans, my experience shaped me and forced me out of my comfort zone.

Growth is important, and learning from mistakes, both mine and others, has always been just as important to me as acquiring knowledge. I realized this one day when my chief pulled me into his office to chat. He showed me a letter signed by our base commander. It was what we called a Letter of Counseling, or LOC. An LOC is one of the first steps in officially counseling someone on their behavior, performance, or other infraction. The Air Force used it as the first level of corrective action, a stern warning that further mistakes or repeated behavior would only yield harsher consequences. It's meant to correct the action and allow the person to recover.

My chief received it because he believed heavily in something, and the base commander disagreed. The two exchanged heated words and both made their points, with the conversation ending on worse terms than when it began.

My chief admitted his tact wasn't correct, but it was necessary. Nobody else in the room was saying the truth, or what the base commander needed to hear, so he did. He believed he owed the base commander an honest opinion, one that he knew would not be popular. It's difficult to call someone out, especially a superior, but it needs to be done. Preferably in a tactful and professional manner. In private is even better.

Nearly thirty years in the military, and this man was still subject to counseling about his performance. It didn't matter that he was a chief, the top rank in the Air Force enlisted tier. Most senior military leaders look toward their senior enlisted men and women for counsel, as it helps them keep the pulse of the enlisted force that they command, as well as balance out leadership. My chief viewed his stripes as a tool. Having obtained the highest enlisted rank possible, he was part of the one percent. Instead of riding that all the way to retirement, he used it to continue to make the Air Force better. In his words, "If I don't use these stripes to do what others can't, and won't, what good are they?"

He further explained to me how the conversation should have gone and how it could have been more productive. What he should have explained to the base commander was his position, along with his concerns to support his position. This alternate approach could have changed the outcome, maybe even convinced the base commander differently. The best part—he took 100% responsibility and couldn't have been humbler about it. A true leader, not afraid of the truth. It was in that moment that I realized the value in telling yourself the truth. Or in hearing the truth. It will never be perfect, but it can be impactful. It won't always be easy to digest, but it is necessary. And you can affect the people you lead. Because whatever you do, don't strive for perfection.

"Perfection is a fool's definition of success."

The above quote is something I said when talking to a colleague one day. After I said it, we both paused, and he said, "That was awesome." I had to write it down. No clue if anyone has ever said it before, but I just blurted it out. *Perfection is a fool's definition of success.* The conversation was regarding results and managing expectations. We had been talking about success and achieving that perfect level of satisfaction in our work, those perfect results. That constant struggle to get that of which we will never acquire... perfection.

Perfection is an impossibility. The goal is not to achieve perfection, but to have a strategy to challenge yourself to obtain results. Behind that challenge is purpose, growth, and knowledge. The aim should be to understand yourself while improving along the way. People still reach for it because our society has painted perfection as a desired outcome instead of a definition. You can't get perfection. It's impossible. And the word perfection has lost its value.

For example, my son loves a good cheese pizza. We've been pursuing the perfect pizza for years. In fact, we've tried hundreds of different pizzas, in many styles, from many places. He's a big critic and never describes things as perfect. For him, perfection is something he's still searching for, something he hasn't experienced yet. We reserve the word for the right time, the right pizza. He's wanting that perfect combination of flavor, crust, cheesiness, and aroma. Despite my best efforts, and the hole in my wallet, we haven't found the perfect pizza yet. But to my son, perfect has a value, and it is something he is still searching for.

We rank pizza on a scale of 1–10. It started because we watched Dave Portnoy, the CEO of Barstool Sports, as he ranked pizza on his social media channels. For Portnoy, ranking pizza and the different styles of pizza was an art form, and he ranks nothing at a 9. If he gives a score of 8.2, that is a solid score, signifying he would eat it again and really, really liked it. It was fun to watch the videos and see what he thought of the different styles and places across the country he visited. We eat plenty of pizzas in my house, so we figured we might as well get on board and do some of our own reviews.

Nothing fancy for us though. No social media videos or YouTube clips. Just a basic pizza review in the Clark family kitchen.

The rules are simple. Everything starts off at about a 6, as that is average pizza comparable to a frozen pizza. It's edible, satisfies the craving, but does little else. It works in a pinch, but there are obviously many better options out there. Below a 6 means we never try it again. Scores of 7-8 are suitable to try again, and we would recommend to a friend. Anything above 8 is damn-near perfect. Above a 9 means we should have invested in the company a long time ago. For the sake of keeping things honest, we stay away from the pizza chains. Nothing against them, but this is a review of local pizza, not corporate America.

When I tell you we've tried hundreds of different pizza places, I'm not joking. We've had some great stuff and some horrible offerings. Our search is still on for the perfect combination of crust, cheese, and sauce. But you know what we learned from all of this? That not only is perfection impossible to find, but you spend a lot of time dedicated to finding it. Time you could use for something else. Plus, nobody in my house really enjoys the same qualities in pizza. My son likes a thicker crust, while my wife prefers a thinner crust and minimal sauce. I like a good zesty sauce, and don't care too much for thin-crusted, floppy pizza. My daughter follows my suit, and from time to time finds something unique that is outside her normal preferences. Regardless, we are still searching for that perfect pizza and having fun while doing it.

Something I came to understand early on was that leadership isn't the pursuit of perfection; rather, it's the pursuit of greatness in others. I don't have all the answers. But I know where I've been, and where I'm going. Better yet, I understand how I got there. It was the leaders before me who paved the way and took the time to ensure that not only did I follow, but that I continued to develop into my own leader and continued to mold future generations of leaders. That means in the future, striving for excellence while knowing perfection isn't a thing to achieve, but is instead a motivator.

Last, the quotes throughout this book are samples from my vast quote collection. I have given credit to specific quotes from specific people. Some quotes have been repeated by multiple people, and therefore are public expressions. To quote everyone who ever said it would fill up an entire book. Finding the originators would be next to impossible, but I would like to acknowledge all of their contributions to the quotes, and the impact those quotes have had.

"I am prepared to go anywhere, provided it be forward."

– David Livingstone

PREPARATION

HERE'S THE TRUTH...

Preparation is undervalued and improperly used.

I CAN NEVER BE TOO PREPARED. Preparation is a comfort for me. I'm a planner and a strategist by nature. I think of scenarios and outline them while planning for contingencies. Call me paranoid or whatever you want but being ready is a comfort.

It could be in part to the anxiety and the panic, which is why planning makes me feel comfortable. It's the predictability that makes me feel better. I eventually realized I was spending tons of time preparing for every scenario I could think of, which was actually consuming my time and adding to my stress. Planning is great in moderation. But I've always believed being ready and prepared is much better than being blindsided or going into something empty-handed.

When I speak about leadership, a big topic I always want to bring up is preparation. In today's fast-paced professional environment, we rarely have adequate time to prepare, and a lot of things suffer because of it. Instead, we rely on confidence to help us navigate, and even the highest levels of confidence can't do what preparation can.

HEAR THESE TRUTHS

> "One important key to success is self-confidence. An important key to self-confidence is preparation."
>
> -Arthur Ashe

Confidence can be more smoke than mirror. Confidence can talk more than our conscience, inflating the feeling and distracting our conscience. There is nothing wrong with having confidence, but we must understand it. Our minds must control how much freedom confidence has, or else confidence will turn into cockiness. Cockiness turns into toxic mentality and often poor decision making. Poor decisions turn into unrepairable consequences, and a good, hard look at the reset button (if someone hasn't already pressed it for you...). Don't let confidence be too much.

I am a firm believer that hitting the reset button is a last resort. It shouldn't be the first answer. Giving up so quickly won't help at all. Grinding it out and enduring through the pain yields results on the other side. Resetting only starts you back at square one, watching everyone else keep moving forward. Nobody ever said the path forward was an easy one. You can, however, prepare for a tough road ahead and endure.

In order to be ready for what this book will cover, I want you to do two things: 1) prepare by understanding purpose, Ikigai, and algorithms; and 2) be honest with yourself. I designed this entire concept around seeing, hearing, and telling the truth.

I reached the levels of success in my career by telling myself the truth, but first I had to hear it. Be honest with yourself and analyze your current take on leadership. Chances are you have room for improvement because everybody does. Ask yourself these questions:

- What do you think you are good at?
- What are you bad at?
- What would you like to improve on?

Now, go ask your peers. Get some feedback from your boss or other prominent leaders. Compare the answers and see if there are any trends or patterns. Don't miss the entire point of growth thinking you already know what to fix. Assuming got nobody anywhere.

What you see isn't what others see, and leadership is about others. No better people to ask than those who follow you. Compared side by side, it might surprise you to what you find and what you need to work on. Humbleness will achieve ultimate growth.

I had a wake-up moment very early in my military career. An outstanding example is a story I'll share. One day my chief pulled me into his office and asked me what I thought held me back. It caught me off guard, but it was a brilliant question. I wasn't totally sure why he asked that of me, but it had to be for a reason. Having been caught off guard, I didn't know what to say, so I just told him, "My leadership." A very general answer, and honestly not my best. The disappointed look on his face confirmed it.

The answer sucked. It was a shot in the dark, with hardly any thought put into it. He then told me my leadership was fine and that he could see plenty of great potential, but my weight was an issue. Back then the Air Force did a waist measurement on you as part of the physical fitness exam. If you had a large waist, or what they deemed as large, it would kill your overall score. You could max out the points on your push-ups, sit-ups, and a one-and-a-half-mile runs, and if your waist was too big, it would hammer you. My chief knew this, and knew I needed to hear the truth.

Now, he didn't tell me I was fat, and I wasn't fat. But I'm a big guy. I'm over two hundred pounds, over six-foot tall, and wear a size twelve shoe. I struggle to buy clothes because over the years XL shirts have become XXL, and I just don't fit or look good in tight shirts. In my prime I was between two hundred twenty-five and two hundred thirty pounds, putting on a few more pounds after I retired (who doesn't?). I'm no NFL lineman, but I'm not small either. This poses problems for guys like me in the Air Force. It's been a controversial subject for years, and something that I think they should have dropped a long time ago. Your waist size doesn't tell anyone how physically fit you are, or if you are capable of physical activity. Not when combined with the other components. The Air Force would never admit it, but the waist measurement wasn't about health or fitness, but how you looked in a uniform.

In combat or emergency situations, it doesn't matter how large or small your waist is. What matters is how you can respond. In all my years of training for contingencies and emergencies, nobody ever stopped and asked me how big around my waist was. Not one person. But they damn sure wanted to know if I could pull someone out of danger and administer first aid. I'm fairly strong for someone my size, and when I was in top shape, I could really move some weights. In an emergency I can drag two people if I have to, but a smaller person might struggle just trying to pull me out of a room. Tell me again how my waist determines my fitness level?

Well, as my chief said, "It's the damn rules, and we have to play within the rules. You don't have to like the rules, but we live in a world where rules are king." And that hit me hard. I needed to work on keeping my weight down or have a backup plan for this military career thing. That level of truth was heavy. I couldn't figure out why he cared about me so much that he would be so honest. Brutal truth does hurt, and sometimes it is necessary. It took me a while to realize what his intent was, and after leaving his office, I figured it out. Leadership is about making others better at your own expense. It's not about you at all. It's about others. He could have easily just watched me fail and shook his head, disappointed that I wasn't better. Instead, he took his own time to shoot it to me straight, ensuring I heard the truth even if I resented him for it. That's why leadership isn't a popularity contest (contrary to what some politicians might think).

The lesson learned was the importance of acceptance. You must hear what others are telling you, because most people don't talk for no reason at all. The truth is hard to hear but needs to be said and heard. The truth you see in the mirror is flawed because it's your view of the truth. A version your mind wants you to see. It's not being honest with you—mirrors never are. I'm talking about the actual truth. The honesty that hurts at first but deep down lights a fire, fueling the heart and mind. Truths that keep you humble and grounded. Although truths hurt to hear, they're the words we need. A wise man can do a lot of good with truths.

"Truth exists. Falsehoods have to be invented."

-Georges Braque

Don't be afraid of those truths. Admit your faults and flaws because not everyone is going to be that honest with you. I told my wife one day, "I care for you enough to hurt your feelings when necessary. Because you can do more with the truth than you can with the lies." You need people around you who will make you better and will do the things necessary to do just that. It's not glamorous at all, but it is necessary. I won't take credit for her success, but some of our best talks came when she doubted herself the most. A hug and reassurance help to soothe the soul, but it jades the mind. I always let her know I was there to support her, but I never held back the truth. Maybe sugarcoated it a little so it was easier to hear, but I never kept from her what I thought would make her better. And she is an excellent physician.

The worst thing you can tell yourself is, "I'm the man." It's bullshit. It's not even close to the truth. Simply an automatic response from your brain when you need it. Naturally we try to protect ourselves, so we say and think things to pump ourselves up. So we end up not telling ourselves the truth for fear of breaking us down further. Instead, we lie to ourselves to obtain false security and confidence.

Why worry about hurting your own feelings? You've got nothing to lose by telling yourself the truth. At that point, the only person to be mad at is yourself, and you better get over that quick. Look in the mirror and say it out loud. That's what I had to do at one point. I couldn't hear the subtle truths from others, so I had to crush my own soul to get it through my thick head (my wife says I'm stubborn). My brain was so busy trying to protect myself from being hurt that it would never hear the truth. Nobody around me was being direct, so I had to say it out loud, in the mirror, staring at myself.

I repeated it multiple times. Each time I stood closer to the mirror and analyzed what I was saying and seeing. After saying it several times, I heard it in someone else's voice. It sunk in, breaking the protective barrier. I can vividly remember it. And it changed my life.

My entire outlook on life changed. It was the first step in becoming something greater. Relieved, like someone had lifted an enormous weight off my shoulders. I was so busy trying to protect myself and justify my actions. But in doing so, I wasn't protecting myself from getting hurt. I was stopping the truth from ever taking hold.

In the pages to follow, I'll explain my concept behind truthful, honest, and humbling leadership. Although it won't be perfect, it will be damn-near, as my father would say. And for me, damn-near is pretty damn good. I took this concept of honest leadership and built it into a philosophy, a purpose, and a vision.

> "Vision is the art of seeing what is invisible."
>
> -Jonathan Swift

While studying for my bachelor's degree in computer science, I heard the term *algorithm*. I didn't know it then, but my studies of computers and networks would eventually help me build a philosophy on leadership.

But first, before we start, we must understand how to build ourselves. Preparing is all in taking the time to read the landscape, take a few deep breaths, and focus your mind on the task at hand. The place you start doesn't matter—what matters is that you start.

I built this concept to fit like an algorithm, which we will talk more in depth on soon. It's a journey to find a comprehensive understanding of your own thoughts and beliefs. Simon Sinek, who preached brilliantly that you need to find your "why," absolutely inspired my development of this leadership algorithm, and I give him massive credit for inspiring me.

So what is an algorithm? An algorithm is a set of rules to obtain an expected output, as shown in the diagram below. Later on, we'll go into deeper detail what an algorithm is, but for now, save this snapshot into your memory:

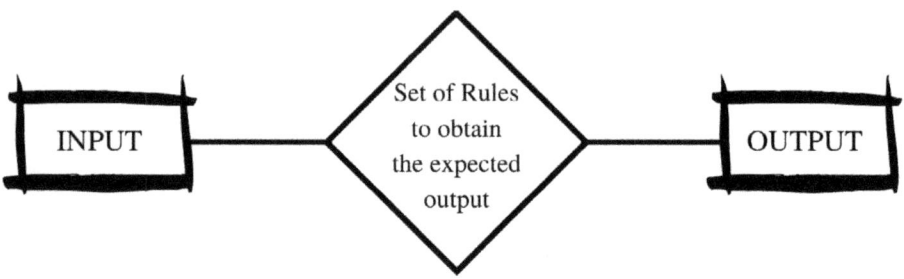

I built my algorithm off of my mission, vision, and purpose. I defined these three things using an *Ikigai,* a Japanese concept meaning "reason of being." This reason of being is essentially why you get up in the morning. Many people would assume that the reason you get up every morning is for money, because money pays the bills. Bills mean food, warmth, and transportation, and require money to have them. Jobs provide money, and without a job, there's no money. No money can equal no food, warmth, or transportation, and that doesn't sound like much fun. Money rules, but it is also just physical. There is a monetary value to it, but not an emotional value. Why you wake up is deeper than money. Money is a byproduct of success, and success is a byproduct of purpose. This understanding defines how you think, feel, and view life. It should be deeper than money.

We spend our lives working for money because that is what we've been taught to do. It's a must. But it is not everything. There is a greater purpose, something that drives you to work for money. Finding it gives you a deeper understanding of why you chase the dollar. Once you find that deeper meaning, you realize that your money works for you; you don't work for it.

PREPARATION

The above Ikigai as my purpose, also known as my "why." Simon Sinek breaks down your "why" in his brilliant book, *Start with Why*, and record-breaking Ted Talk. It is such groundbreaking stuff that I read the book twice, and I've watched the Ted Talk a million times.

Instead of using that exact formula here, I went with the Ikigai. Why? Well, because for me it's easier to explain. To start, you just have to define your 1) mission, 2) vision, and 3) goals. Together, those form your purpose and create a purpose statement. When I developed this for myself, I just wrote a paragraph of my thoughts. I used the Ikigai because I'm a visual person, and I could visually tear parts out of the paragraph and place them in the diagram. An old military term we used to use was KISS (Keep It Simple Stupid), so keeping it simple and breaking it down with a visual helped me understand it better. Do it however you want, but those three things above are what you need.

"Success is where persistence meets preparation."

ALGORITHMS

HERE'S THE TRUTH...

Leadership is the simplest, most complex, and diverse thing in the world.

GETTING STARTED AS A LEADER is maybe the biggest uphill battle you'll ever professionally face. Lord knows I struggled with it. It's funny because we think that as leaders, people will just move when we say move, but people are intellectuals and will question everything, especially from the inexperienced. And you can say "move" a thousand times until you are blue in the face, but if you don't say it with tact, experience, and purpose, nobody will ever listen.

Leadership is a complex subject nearly impossible to perfect. Anybody that tells you differently is lying. It will feel as if there are no right answers, yet plenty of wrong ones. Perfecting it will feel like your greatest failure. It's frustrating, confusing, and time-consuming. Keeping your head above water is a struggle, and we continue to tread to avoid drowning. We can never stay ahead of the game because we never truly understand the game being played, or we make moves to stay ahead of the game and put the cart before the horse. What we did incorrectly was take the wrong first step. Leadership isn't merely a concept you just do; it's something you live, breathe, and understand. In order to stay ahead of the game, you must understand the game you are playing.

Yes, leadership can be full of successes, failures, and lessons learned. Approaching it without a strategy will bury you and slow progress. You will fail more often than not, and your peers and subordinates will quickly lose faith in you. Fake it until you make it is not a good philosophy in leadership. Authentic and genuine actions will foster growth and development while playing the long game.

We widely recognize Michael Jordan as the greatest player to ever play professional basketball. We have chronicled his life and playing career in just about every magazine or news publication in existence. When he played, you either hated or loved him, and sometimes both. But he was a winner, a leader on the court. Nothing summed it up better than when ESPN released a documentary about him called *The Last Dance*. The documentary really revealed how tough Jordan was on his teammates. The level of performance he demanded on the court was insane and speaks to why he led his team to six championships. They shot the documentary interview-style to capture Jordan's reaction to other people's comments and get his insight on certain parts of his career. In one interview for the documentary, Jordan said this about leadership:

> "Winning has a price. Leadership has a price. I pushed people when they didn't wanna be pushed. I challenged people when they didn't wanna be challenged. But I never asked them to do something I wasn't willing to do myself."
>
> - *Michael Jordan*

Jordan had a purpose. He knew that although he was often the highest scorer, as well as the highest paid player on the team, he had a responsibility as a leader. His leadership drove others to greatness with him. He had a concept of leadership, a personal philosophy about how he played the game. He had a plan, and things either fell into that plan or they didn't. Adjustments were made, but he maintained a relentless pursuit of greatness.

As I learned more about technology and how it has shaped the internet, I realized the internet was built and maintained with a purpose, as are leaders. And because I can be a bit of a tech nerd, I figured why not compare the two? And honestly, you can't build a website without a purpose, and you can't answer those three questions above without a strategy. That tech strategy is in the algorithms and code. Your

ALGORITHMS

leadership strategy is all in the mission, vision, and goals. Combined, it creates your formula for success and defines your purpose in action.

Purpose is important because we have to have a road map to follow. You don't go on a road trip without directions, do you? Most of us don't because we'll get lost. We need instructions and rules to complete the task and make it to our destination. An algorithm is just that, a set of rules and/or directions to be followed in calculations or problem-solving processes.

A formula is a road map to success. It guides you, inspires you, and keeps you in between the lines. In tech, algorithms do the same, keeping true to the defined purpose. That's the formula. Almost every major platform on the web has an algorithm, with websites using them to drive traffic, filter content, and keep the blood pumping throughout the site. It's critical to the success. Algorithms are everywhere.

Why do we have all of this? Well, because of search engines like Google. Google uses a thing called Search Engine Optimization (SEO), which is a smart platform that filters and finds web content. It crawls deep throughout the web, finding unique content and ranking it according to what the world wants to see now. Mastering SEO is a large key to success today and having a search engine ranking all but guarantees it. Algorithms are rule sets and processes for success. By following this strategy—creating great code and algorithms that drive your purpose—you've created a formula for success. In your leadership you need the same, as flying by the seat of your pants simply doesn't work.

In reality, leaders are search engines like Google. They are an open source of information. Outstanding leaders have endless amounts of knowledge and information that can be shared. And with the right search engine, that information can be found and shared. But once you've found information you have to do something with it, and that is where algorithms come in. Just telling people information only goes so far. Explaining, curating, and executing that information makes people believers. For example, I know a Mercedes is a nice car, but I'll never truly know it until I drive one. The experience is unique and differs from the image I see. Once I get behind the wheel and can put my hands on the leather interior, witness the quietness of the cabin, and feel the smooth ride of the suspension, I'll really know how nice a Mercedes is.

Today, you can build a personal blog for free through many web hosts. It's never been easier to write, create, and post content. There are hundreds of websites that will allow you to build your own personal blog. Do you desire to expand that blog into selling books, advertisements, and other products? There's a little thing called plug-ins that allow you to create those ads, and others to help you create a store to sell those products. All online. But you won't appear in search results until you have mastered SEO and understand the algorithms. Your leadership needs the same thing. It has to be more than a concept or strategy. It has to have a method to be used, or it's just a pretty website with no functionality. Information is no good unless we can find it.

Picture this: Google giving you a top ranking. What would that do for your business or blog? I picture it being a lot like Scrooge McDuck when he dives into the big tank full of money. You want to be on the front search page of Google, not the second page. Nobody cares about the second page. The name of the game today is SEO and beating the algorithms. So getting your content SEO-compatible has created entire businesses looking to optimize SEO and create perfect algorithm-friendly content. And without SEO, your content is a no-go. It's going to be pretty hard to be successful when your content is a dud. Get the picture? Like a website hoping to be found by a search engine like Google, your leadership must be developed to be not only valuable, but also discovered.

Why did I tell you all of this? Because SEO and the algorithms are the gatekeepers to all of this content. And like the internet, leadership needs its own algorithm, and you need a gatekeeper to your own ideals, values, and concepts. This entire process has grown, and people want more but it's under lock and key, creating even more demand.

Same goes for leadership. Not only do we strive to understand it, master it, and display it, but so do our subordinates. The audience craves more intimate leadership content, and creating it is a time-consuming process. It's a struggle as a leader to master something that frankly isn't obtainable; the same goes for our subordinates. Your staff will strive to understand their leader—you—who is constantly changing because of your own duties. It's a frustrating battle of trying to figure it all out. As leaders, we battle to understand the rules of leadership.

The formula to constructing a great algorithm, i.e., your purpose-driven rule sets, is hearing the truth. Remember, the formula for an algorithm is inputs, sets of rules, and expected outputs. To build an algorithm, you must understand those principles and be truthful with yourself. You will never design a good algorithm for yourself if the vision of its contents is jaded. The results won't be optimal, and they will leave you wondering what happened.

ALGORITHMS

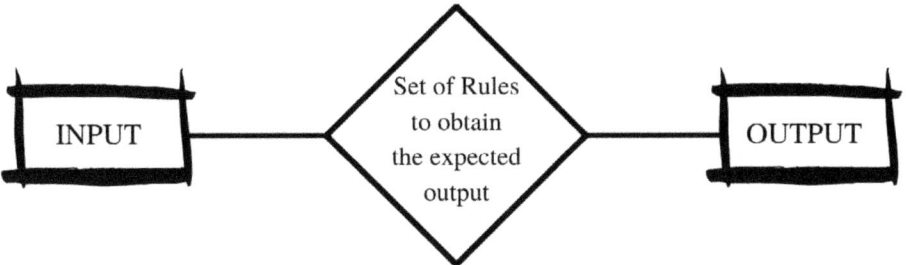

This authentic and honest approach to building this philosophy has to be pure, free of bias. Just like an algorithm guides people through the content of a website, your school of thought on leading must do the same. It's the call to action. The user's experience needs to be tailored to them, and the algorithm does that. To summarize, we build honest and authentic leaders through definition, understanding, and rule sets that guide our actions. A deliberate approach to leadership that is the most effective. *A leadership algorithm.*

Now, like an algorithm, your leadership must be flexible. We'll talk more about flexibility later. Flexibility is a big part of being a leader.

We adjust algorithms all the time as technology advances and the world shifts. The beautiful thing about algorithms is the functional way they exist in our lives, tailoring the experience in how we use the internet, and what we get out of the experience. A website succeeds or fails based upon whether the user found the content useful, or not useful at all. If it wasn't what they were looking for, they will move on and keep looking. So, the algorithm must be fine-tuned from time to time.

> "Perhaps the most important principle of a good algorithm is the refusal to be content."
>
> -Alfred V. Aho

The thing to understand is that this won't be the last plan you ever put together. These social media websites and search engines constantly update their algorithms to stay current. Instead of trying to predict what is going to happen, they try to direct what is going to happen. The entire purpose of an algorithm is to show you the results they want you to see, based on a customized experience. That's why when you Google "iPhone cases," the ads on your social media sites then show iPhone-related accessories like phone cases. The algorithm is pulling information from one place and using it to customize your experience in another place. They aren't predicting anything; rather, they are directing it in real time. Literally putting things in front of your eyes that they know you already want to see, and making you see them again until that experience is converted into a sale. That's how the internet became so monetized. There are literally billions of dollars on the internet. For you, as a leader, you need to do the same. Put in front of people exactly what they want to see, multiple times, until you finally sell them on it.

Those users who do figure out those algorithms and try to cheat the system often get punished. It's been widely rumored that the major social media sites will throttle back your experience if you try to cheat the algorithm. While doing some research, I came across the term "shadow-banned." It's basically where you try to cheat the algorithm into thinking your profile on a social media site is more popular than what it really is, and once you are caught, the platform throttles you back and slows down your growth. The less time you spend on their site, the more they will show your content (pictures, videos, etc.) to others in order to lure you back to spend more time. Also, the more attention your content gets, the more the algorithm will show it to more people, further expanding your reach. If the algorithm thinks you are cheating and getting automated likes or expanded views, it will throttle you back. The goal is organic and authentic content, content interaction, and the user experience. It's a delicate balance.

Keep this in mind as you build your own algorithm, except in this case, you want to share your leadership algorithm with others, have them get more and more out of you, and always be ready to adjust and change it. We won't be punishing or "shadow-banning" anybody for understanding our algorithm, but we also won't be complacent about it either. Clear as mud, right?

Last, since you know this, don't try to predict what will happen. People who try to get ahead of the algorithm spend more time trying to figure it out and cheat it, instead of understanding and using it. You want to manipulate the algorithm? Use it for what it's for instead of trying to break the code. Major websites like Facebook, Instagram, and Twitter don't share their algorithms on purpose. Neither does Google. It isn't shared because it will keep you spending more and more time on the site trying to master it. And that time spent with them makes them money.

I built my own personal algorithm based on my experiences, successes, failures, and my personality, as well as many late nights reading up on algorithms, SEO, and how these platforms all work. This algorithm defines my vision, mission, goals, and outlook. The confidence it creates within me is unexplainable. It's simple and easy, yet elegant and sophisticated at the same time. It defines what it takes to achieve success while not overthinking it. Your Efforts define your work ethic and how hard you will work. The Process is the processes, steps, and actions needed to achieve an output. And last, Progress is the combination of the two, or your results and outputs. My basis for this book, and my leadership mentality...

$$\text{Effort + Process = PROGRESS}$$

POWER OF PURPOSE

<u>HERE'S THE TRUTH...</u>
Power doesn't make you a leader. Understanding purpose does.

A COMMON MYTH I'VE SEEN in people throughout my career is that they felt a powerful grasp on power would solidify their leadership. And they were wrong. Although power is something you can obtain, getting it doesn't mean you are powerful. Power grabs are on full display within our government and elected officials. If you aren't already tuned in, the political fighting in Washington isn't over policies and laws—it's over the power to make the policies and laws. Each party has an agenda, and each party wants the power to push their agenda through until it is law. And each party wants to make laws that prevent the other party from obtaining the power to override their new laws, and it has turned into a vicious circle that we the people have to deal with every four years. Politics is a nightmare, and it's because it's shifted from being about purpose and to being about obtaining power.

Purpose guides you, drives you, and helps you understand your actions. We must understand purpose in order to understand leadership. Being an excellent leader is powerful and purposeful. The algorithm you design will only work when the purpose is understood, by both you and the people you serve. Never be afraid to explain your purpose to others and challenge them to explain their purpose. If they can't, walk them through it and help them find it. Exemplary leaders help others find purpose, and they aren't concerned with power. You want genuine power? Find purpose in what you do, and help others find their purpose. The influence you will have over people will be so impactful that it will change their outlook, maybe even their lives, and that will be a powerful thing.

While conducting research for my website design, I was told a magnificent piece of advice from a website developer. He said something that really struck me. When it comes to building a website, there are three things you want to answer when a customer visits your website:

1. What do you do?
2. What can you do to make their life better?
3. How do they buy from you?

In his expert opinion, these three things need to be clear when someone visits your site. They should be blatantly obvious. I found myself going to several of my favorite websites, and even my own, and seeing if this was true. Could I answer all three of these questions? More often than not, I found the answer to be yes. The smart money is on making sure you offer this info up immediately when someone visits your website. It doesn't matter if you are an author, a business, or running a blog. These questions need to be answered or else the viewer/reader won't stick around. For websites, it's called *bounce rate*.

Bounce rate is an internet marketing term used in analytical website evaluation. It measures how long a single-person session lasts on a single page of your website, divided by all the other sessions from previous visitors. This rate is important because it measures how long someone sticks around while not taking any action. They haven't clicked any links, filled out any forms, or made a purchase. Essentially, bounce rate tells you how long people stay on your website. Bounce rate significantly helps answer the three questions noted above, and further explains why they are so important. As a leader, I don't want a high bounce rate. I want a low one, because I want to be engaging. I want people to *want* to listen to me and to stick around. Your website bounce rate equals how effective your site is at capturing and keeping their attention, and the same applies to your leadership.

This concept toward building a website is interesting, as it delivers almost immediately. The point is to capture the audience and keep them interested and provided with value. In fact, I was surprised at first at how complex the concept was, and then I realized that it was actually quite simple and effective. I visited a bunch of websites and asked those three questions above. I could answer them on a multitude of websites, both sales and professional sites. And the more I thought about it, the more I realized that *leadership should be that obvious*. And that's when it hit me: technology and leadership today are not so different. As a leader, I really want these same things being asked of me, and I want to be providing answers. I want people to engage with me and to be provided value. I want to them to stick around and look for more info, all while being fulfilled in what they've seen so far. Tech and leadership concepts aren't so different. Follow me here—don't get too lost in the tech talk.

As a leader, I want to be open, honest, and obvious. I want to state my intentions and my expectations clearly and leave no doubt. When there are questions about you, there will be unsureness amongst the people who follow you.

You want to answer those three questions from above as a leader. Your subordinates, or team, should be able to answer those questions when talking about you.

WHAT DO YOU DO?

He's a leader. Takes care of me when I need help or helps when I am getting frustrated. Walks the walk and talks the talk. Demands high expectations from me, and even higher from himself. Portrays a selfless leader who always has my back, and constantly asks me to grow, learn, and even lead myself.

WHAT CAN YOU DO TO MAKE THEIR LIFE BETTER?

He allows me to focus on my work. The established communication lines allow for efficient updates so he as the boss can stay updated while not killing my momentum. He adds to the conversation and supports us. I'm not scared to talk to him or bring new ideas to the table. Last, he's flexible and takes care of me. He's not penny-pinching or watching the clock. I know that if I need to leave work early, he trusts that it's for a good reason and makes sure my home life is priority #1.

HOW DO THEY BUY FROM YOU?

He leads by example. He has not asked me to do something that he himself wasn't willing to do either. I've seen him roll up his sleeves and get his hands dirty plenty of times and make the sacrifice when needed. He's flexible and sets the example. I want to follow him for who he is and what he stands for. Listening is a priority because he provides value, knowledge, and support. I'm "buying" from him because he leads with purpose, respect, and drive. It's always value-added. He's a servant leader who I *want* to follow.

The above are examples of how someone would answer those questions regarding me as a leader. I didn't make those up. I actually polled my coworkers and asked them how they would answer them when thinking of me. After consolidation it revealed some great insights, as well as patterns and trends. The feedback was invaluable, and it's something people don't prioritize enough when in leadership positions.

If you want to know the truth, ask the questions. And this level of feedback can be crucial to growing as a leader. If they can provide deep and thoughtful responses, that is a good thing! But if they can't, or need time to think, you haven't affected them enough yet, or it scared them to tell the truth. But, with a thorough understanding of Power and Purpose you leave that impression on them.

So, let's really break down the purpose of power. There is no power in leadership. Those who think otherwise aren't leaders; they are managers and bosses, and those are two very different things. What they've done is let the idea of power consume them and jade their vision. Pure strength and control are what they desire. Control is important to them, more so than influence, as they think power will influence others. Technically they are correct, but they assume power will positively influence people and, in reality, a show of power almost always intimidates and asks the individual or individuals to react negatively.

For example, anytime Russia flies a bomber close to the Alaskan coast in international waters as a show of force, the US scrambles several fighter jets out of Elmendorf or Eielson Air Force Base. The US has stationed their most advanced fighters up in Alaska to counter this potential power. Keep in mind the US sends up a multi-million dollar fifth-generation fighter in the F-22 Raptor to intercept a Russian TU-95 Bear bomber that still uses propellers and has been in service with Russia since the early 1950s. They respond to a showcase of power with even more advanced power.

Now, the missile warning systems go nuts and everybody watches the radar like a hawk. The US is ready to strike if that bomber poses a threat. A display of power, met with a reaction of equal or greater power. Although this act is completely within the rights of Russia, as it is in international waters or according to an agreement between Russia and the US, it's still a display of power. You flex your muscles, and it will cause someone else to do so in return, often in a larger or more impressive manner. And what does it accomplish? Nothing really, just each country showing off their power.

Dynamic leaders understand that the true power lies in the ability to influence, impress, and inspire, not flex their muscles. The most difficult thing for a lot of leaders is getting a deep understanding of power. Nobody really has a grasp of power like they should. It's not what you think it is. Standing over someone as the boss isn't power; it's intimidation. And, power and leading ARE NOT the same, and shouldn't be compared or used together. Power is for individuals with egos, like politicians and celebrities who use it to get what they want and sit in their ivory towers. It's not really power, but rather a false sense of it. Leadership isn't about power, but it can be powerful.

The issue with power is that leaders think it's something that can be gained, simply bought from the store. That alone shows how they value power. It can't be obtained. That false sense of obtaining power easily is entirely what is wrong with American politics today. It's all about power and using it over people. Calling all the shots, speaking on behalf of everyone, and ignoring the truth. Nothing frustrates me more than American politics. I'd love to teach a leadership class one day solely on American politics, as it's full of things NOT to do. It's become a large dictatorship where the few in Washington make all the decisions for the majority and tell them how to live their lives. They stand up there in the sacred halls, keep tons of secrets and provide only the narrative they want us to know. It's the opposite of leadership, and the last time someone stood up over a country and tried to force power over people a lot of bad things happened.

Instead, power should be viewed as an asset, a motivating tool like a symphony maestro. Ever hear John Williams conduct an orchestra? It's beautiful, powerful, and majestic. He moves his hands and that baton (that's the little stick thing) with precision, guiding the musicians to a masterpiece. He's not the most powerful person on stage, he's simply the one organizing it all. The power is in the instruments being played by the experts dedicated to the music. It's art. John Williams can't play all those instruments at once and he knows it, but he also knows how to leverage powerful people and lead them to a masterpiece, which is why he is considered one of the best composers ever.

Power is uplifting and should be used as a motivator, not as an intimidator. Power over people has historically not gone over well. The most effective leaders in history were often not designated leaders at all. They didn't hold political offices or command massive armies. Although, if you look back at the very early US and world wars and study how their leaders conducted battle, you will see how influential they were. But they were also on the front lines with the troops, getting their hands dirty. Today, these leaders command from the comfort of secure facilities, fancy offices, and a gigantic mansion in Washington.

I defined my purpose by using an *Ikigai*, a Japanese diagram meaning "reason of being." This diagram allowed me to outline my key priorities in just a few words. Now when we talk about power, understanding our purpose and being able to speak about it is much more powerful than a show of power or having power over people. True power over people is the ability to inspire, influence, and uplift. Power yielded without a true understanding of its purpose can be very dangerous. Nobody with power who used it for their own purposes ever came out on top. Those who use power for the greater good and for the betterment of others typically find much more success.

Throughout this book, we will discuss many powerful things and how to use them correctly. Being aware of the power in leadership and the purpose of power divides the leaders from the managers. At this point you can go get your golf clubs or keep reading. The choice is yours, but it sends a powerful message, regardless.

I said the below quote during a conversation with someone in regard to talking about things we were passionate about. People often talk about passion and confuse it for purpose. This person was talking about things they were passionate about, but when asked about their progress they had no response. That's because we don't always relate passion to our purpose. I'm passionate about a lot of things, but I don't do them for a profession. Those things have nothing to do with my purpose in life. Amateurs talk about passion and don't follow through. Professionals turn passions into purposes, and purposes into results.

> "Passion is for amateurs, focus on purpose."

PART I
EFFORT

<u>EFFORT</u> + Process = Progress

The first part of the algorithm is EFFORT. Effort as defined by Webster's dictionary is:

effort (noun)
1. Conscious exertion of power: hard work
2. A serious attempt: TRY
3. Something produced by exertion or trying

Effort separates us from everyone else. Effort wins championships, seals deals, and is a key element of success. Just showing up and trying is half the battle. This quote is something I've always lived by:

> "If you try and fail, congratulations. Most people won't even try."
>
> — *Albert Einstein*

Why is this quote so important to me? Well, because leaders have to try. In this section we will discuss the first part of the algorithm I've built: EFFORT. This section will focus heavily on showing up, trying, and putting in the time to be effective. This is the first part of the algorithm simply because putting forth an effort is better than putting forth nothing at all. Without at least an attempt, you can't build, learn, and grow. The entire point of the algorithm is to grow, adapt, and mature.

So, putting forth an effort helps the process get started, because we have to have faith in the processes in order to achieve results. In any organization—regardless of size—faith in the culture, processes, and leadership must be apparent, or else effort will die across the board. You, as a leader, must give people a reason to give forth effort.

Effort is an overarching, holistic concept that is hard to define and even harder to contain. But what can't be contained can also be lost, or never provided. That's why you have to give it GAS (Give A Shit). Effort doesn't just come easily; it's a grind and often a thankless, results-lacking, big time pain in the ass, but that's what makes leadership so exceptional. Leadership isn't about you, it's about others.

The level of effort can determine the results, and since we are putting effort into the processes (next section of the algorithm), it's safe to assume that weak effort into any process is going to result in weak results. I don't know about you, but I'm not about weak results. I need big results, with quality effort and input.

In the chapters that follow, we are going to talk heavily about how effort affects your leadership and how it will change the outcome of the algorithm. This section is critically important as we take the first step in truly understanding who we are as leaders and how what we "input" into our leadership creates an influential output.

Effort is where success starts. Bottom line… you have to give it GAS.

CHAPTER I

LEADERSHIP

HERE'S THE TRUTH...

You can't lead by example if you aren't the example.

"DO AS I SAY, NOT AS I DO," is the biggest load of crap I've ever heard. How can you lead people while going against your own advice and guidance? As professionals, we often catch ourselves overthinking way too often. And usually it's about stuff that we don't need to be thinking that much about. We have a natural reaction to overcomplicate and overthink things. It's a habit born out of stress and pressure, and one that all leaders should fully know. That's when we say one thing but mean another. Leadership is already an enormous challenge; don't make it more confusing.

You will not get people to change their habits until you start telling the truth and keeping it simple for yourself. Don't speak until you practice what you preach, as saying one thing and doing another is the fastest track to losing credibility.

When I was teaching, I used this approach as when mentoring and counseling my students. In order to preach to them about trusting their gut, keeping things simple, and listening to their first instinct, I had to also do it myself. Overthinking and second-guessing are killers for decision making, in or out of the classroom. Providing prominent examples was always the key. If I had a student who was unsure of how to approach a test question, I would ask them random questions and not provide any options for answers. I would ask them what their gut was saying to them, and then we walked through it. At least half the time they were already in the right direction from the start. Once they learned to trust their gut, they had a better-than-fifty-percent success rate. Closer to eighty or ninety percent. Instincts don't lie.

It applies in a variety of situations, and it's a huge part of leadership. We often ask leaders to make decisions, sometimes without all the information, or sometimes with an overabundance of information. And of course, with never enough time to analyze it all. What's worse? Too much or too little? Either way, it doesn't really matter because you should be half-cocked anyway and ready to pull the trigger. Listening to yourself and going with your instincts are going to lead you in the right direction more often than not.

> "Trust your hunches. They're usually based on facts filed away just below the conscious level."
>
> — Joyce Brothers

But we must be truthful leaders. We have to stop sugarcoating our thoughts and start speaking the truth. With leadership, a powerful voice knows how to tell people exactly what they need to hear. A lot of the times that is the truth, and the truth doesn't always feel good. But talented leaders know and understand how to tell the truth without being vulgar or brash or too blunt or subjective. It's something we will touch on later when talking about communication. Leaders know and understand how to say it in a manner that conveys realism, honesty, and genuine concern.

Leadership is that thing, that quality, that people have that influences the surrounding people. Leadership has no title. It has no status. It has no popularity. If you are looking for those things, then you are a manager, a boss, and you likely have an ego. Those things don't come with being a leader. Those might be perks of the job, but they aren't qualities of a leader. The mindset of great leadership is simple and concise in its aim to influence, motivate, and inspire.

My philosophy of leadership is very simple. You selflessly push people to greatness because that's the right thing to do. It's not selfish, ego-driven, or about the recognition. It's about empowering people to be the natural, outstanding version of themselves. A result of those efforts is often some sort of recognition, but that's a result, and we aren't chasing those kinds of results.

An all-encompassing guide to leadership doesn't exist. There's no book that has all the rules, no perfect steps to take. But there is an entire world of knowledge out there, and plenty of lessons to learn. Instead of trying to mimic someone else, model your mainframe off of lessons learned and the people who have come before you. And one of the best lessons I ever learned from a leader who came before me was TACT.

Tact will kill a conversation before it even starts. Your tact, and how you approach a conversation or a hard decision, will determine how that conversation goes, how that decision is made, and what people think of their interaction with you. Bad tact means a likely unfavorable outcome. A good approach, with a tactful voice and meaningful conversation, heavily increases the likelihood of a favorable outcome. Tact is not something everyone is blessed with, and sometimes it just has to be learned.

Why? Well, because we don't hear ourselves very well, if at all. It's hard to hear yourself talk, even if you enjoy hearing yourself talk. That's because we don't hear our own emotions in our own voice. We hear those words, how we want to hear them, and how we want them to be heard. But as we will talk later about communication, you can't force someone to hear it your way.

Tact and approach are huge in a relationship, and the best example is probably marriage and partnerships. We are used to how we sound, and so is the other person. That's why your voice sounds wrong when you hear it in a recording. You've been conditioned to your version of your voice. So when you start a conversation and you want it to go a certain way, just remember that other person doesn't hear the tone, emotion, and sincerity that you are hearing in your head. In order to get around this, think about what you are going to say before you say it. This isn't an elementary thing for outgoing and vocal people, and it especially hits introverts differently. Marriages and relationships/partnerships are often, but not always, a combination of two people who AREN'T exactly alike. It's true, opposites do often attract. So an extrovert might be in a relationship with an introvert. Their method of communication is very dynamic because one likes to talk and socialize, while the other might not. Each one has a different tactful approach to conversations, decision making, and addressing conflict.

As a leader, you will have a workplace or organization full of people with all kinds of personalities, backgrounds, and preferences. Talking to all of them effectively is nearly impossible. Pleasing everyone is a pointless pursuit of perfection. However, you can master your tact and approach to achieve maximum effectiveness.

It's something that I worked on earlier in my career. If I didn't like something, or I didn't like somebody, or I just didn't like a process, I would say so. I didn't have any tact about it. There was no strategy in how I delivered it. And I when I first became a supervisor, it was my Achilles heel. I would just tell people when they screwed up or did something wrong. No tactful approach, no honest feedback, no empowering advice, or a slap on the back. Just a simple, negative criticism and walk away.

I thought I was being honest, and that people would appreciate that honesty. I couldn't have been more wrong. Fortunately, I had a great supervisor at the time who pulled me into his office one day and told me I was a jerk and an asshole, and I was tough to listen to. I thought it was pretty rude, considering he was supposed to be someone I looked up to. Then he hit me with this: "Now, how did that feel?"

What happened next was a lesson in listening while you lead. I wasn't allowed to talk or respond. My task was just to listen. He then told me over the course of almost an hour that although I was trying to lead, I wasn't coming across as a leader. I was coming across as a boss. And that is the day I learned the difference. And every day since then I've made sure the people who worked for me understood it too.

Here's what you can do with the truth to make it a little easier for people to swallow and understand. Be tactful about it. My supervisor in the above example told me in an hour what he probably could have told me in less than ten minutes. But it wasn't about being quick; it was about being heartfelt and meaningful. Sometimes that takes time, especially when you are delivering a big truth that will change someone or hit them emotionally. Because pain will leave once it's done teaching you.

It's okay to tell people the truth, but you need to follow the truth up with strategic and intentional calls to action. If you're going to tell somebody that they're not doing a good job or that they need to do better, you also need to follow up with how to do it. Empower them to make those changes for the better and leave them with a call to action.

Give them ammo for the fight. Nothing is worse for an aspiring leader than trying to figure it all out for themselves. Toss some ideas out there. "Have you ever thought about x? Have you tried doing z?"

Getting down to the root of the problem is necessary too, so don't be afraid to ask them how the situation went or what they thought of it. "How did you feel about this process? Did you have enough tools to do the job? Did you have enough support and resources? Enough guidance?" And even ask them to give themselves feedback. "What feedback would you provide yourself about that?" Turning the tables on them in an active discussion gives aspiring leaders a new perspective, one that you can also help guide and influence.

Lessons learned don't happen if lessons aren't taught.

So, if you were to switch the algorithm around, you'll see that progress happens when processes and effort combine. You have to look at both sides of the equation. If you get a poor result (progress), walk it all backwards and see where the misstep was (in the processes or effort?). Finding out what we did wrong is much easier than trying to find out why the listener heard it wrong. For starters, they might not even be willing to tell you to your face that it was horrible, or what turned them off. So, finding those things out and getting straightforward answers actually isn't easy at all!

You can see why listeners heard it wrong if you watch their body language and reactions. And people who try to lead go in the wrong direction because they take the easy way out and blame the people listening instead of blaming themselves. There is no level of self-accountability, no self-blame, just passing of the blame on to the listener. And blaming the listener is a ticket-punch on the fast track to losing credibility as a leader.

Tact is the beginning step of showcasing leadership. In history there have been some influential leaders who started off horribly wrong. They had no tact, or very little of it. The first sentence that came out of their mouth turned people off, and now those people won't listen again. You only get one chance to make a great first impression. After that, you must climb a mountain without a rope to earn it back.

In my career I had good and bad leaders, with some of those bad leaders just needing to reevaluate their approach and their tact. Those leaders had great intention, great ideas, and great energy. But instead of delivering leadership to the listener, they tried to connect the listener to the leader. They got it the wrong way around. You can't force the listener to connect to the leader. That connection must come naturally. Your job as a leader is to connect to them, giving them a reason and value-added purposes to connect to you.

Be strategic and purposeful in your leadership, and you'll make more connections just by being authentically you.

CHAPTER 2

SELF-LICKING ICE CREAM CONE

HERE'S THE TRUTH...

Leaders are not the center of attention. And never should be.

PICTURE AN ICE CREAM CONE for a minute. It looks great, very desirable. Probably very delicious. It serves a purpose—to satisfy that sweet tooth, that craving. It's consumed in a manner that brings joy and self-fulfillment. Or at least that's how it should be. I've never seen someone eat ice cream and not be happy about it.

Bureaucracy can be a nightmare. It can be the most useful resource when it works correctly, and the most useless thing when it doesn't. It can be stale, uncreative, and inept. Pete Worden said it perfectly in a 1992 paper when describing the organization at NASA. It's a *self-licking ice cream cone*. In other words, it's a self-perpetuating system that has no purpose other than to sustain itself.

I heard this term many times while in the military. I met leaders who exemplified it. Almost like they lived and breathed it. A commanding officer who knew so little that they were too afraid to admit it and just made up leadership as they went on. It made them feel good, as they were the ones in charge. They had no purpose, and to justify their lack of purpose, they made things up to justify their own existence.

HEAR THESE TRUTHS

Unfortunately, this can be the case all too often in an organization or certain people groups. Politicians come to mind.

Having a team that can perform well on its own is fantastic and a sign of good management. But it's not the end. There's more to it than that. Managers need to know what to do once the team performs. Standing around with your hands in your pockets won't cut it, because the team will eventually need help to take the next step. You have to develop with the team. Serve a purpose.

If you don't know what you are doing, that is fine. It happens all the time. Let go of your ego and ask for help. Ask for suggestions. Lean on your senior employees. Just don't make stuff up because you are without purpose or direction.

In the movie *Talladega Nights,* Will Ferrell plays Ricky Bobby, a famous race car driver who is pretty goofy. He wins a few races and has to do an interview. Because he's new, he doesn't know how to conduct himself or what to do with his hands. During the interview, he awkwardly stands with his hands up around his chest. At one point he even says, "I don't know what to do with my hands." The scene itself is hilarious but is also a sign that nobody coached him on what to do. It was time for him to take the next step in success and nobody was around to guide him. It was a failure on the team to support the face of the organization.

In this scenario, he was on a major team, surrounded by professionals. Plenty of resources at his disposal, yet nobody around to use them. As the driver, he did his job and he won the race. The crew did their jobs and kept the car in top condition all race long. The result: big victory. But he couldn't have looked worse in that interview.

The purpose of the rest of the team is to support the driver. Be there to handle the public relations, sponsors, and other media requests. All while coaching the driver on how to talk to the media, represent the sponsors, and engage with the fans. Your job as a leader is much the same. Show up, provide value, and be purposeful.

The problem with leaders is that they do a great job of supporting the team, providing info, guidance, and direction, but then they stop. That's it. Job done, high five to me!

Nope, wrong. That is what you are *supposed* to do. Now it's time to be more than that and be a leader.

This is when the job starts. The fun has only just begun. And this is exactly where leaders get in trouble. When it's time to put up or shut up, management disappears and all you hear is crickets. Well, what good are you when the team achieves great things, and you can't tell them what to do next? Or what direction to go in? Momentum? Who cares about momentum? Now you are a self-licking ice cream cone. Momentum is dead, and at this point you are only good for your own good. Only there to sustain yourself, justify your own existence. And employees hate that. You haven't given them the value they need, and you serve no purpose. The only person patting you on the back is yourself.

Instead, the role of manager is of a servant leader, in place to watch the team rise to greatness and continue to challenge them. To take charge and steer the ship. Be there when the going gets tough and the team needs guidance. Not to justify the job title, big salary, and corner office.

My approach to managing people was simple. If the team did all of this work without you, achieved all these fantastic results without you, then why do they need you? If you've had no impact on their performance, other than supporting their work, what have you really done? What purpose do you serve?

The point is this: you are replaceable. I can put a job posting out there for a mid-level manager, say around $75,000 per year with good benefits, and probably get a dozen applicants. I can hire a new manager and teach them how I want them to lead. What I can't do is replace the momentum and cohesion that a team has worked hard to build.

I hired many people in my career, and the one thing I looked for in all of them was how they would lead. It didn't matter what the position was for—a sign of leadership is a sign that they can work with a team. Because leaders understand that sometimes they have to be a leader and sometimes have to be a follower. I don't need self-licking ice cream cones. I need leaders, and so does your team.

> "What you do has far greater impact than what you say."
>
> — Stephen Covey

Picture a self-licking ice cream cone. It sounds like the most ridiculous thing in the world. Just a self-serving, endless circle of nothing. It's almost like a fountain, just recirculating the water so that the waterfall continues to look nice. It's fun to look at, and that's about it. Serves no purpose other than aesthetics.

In leadership, we have to play the long game and trust the process, but first, we must put forth the effort and understand that leadership is about others, not ourselves. So how you act today will determine the results a year from now. Act accordingly.

An outstanding example is Steve Balmer, the CEO of Microsoft back in the early 2000s. Steve Balmer was the CEO of Microsoft back when the big tech wars had just started heating up. Apple, Google, Microsoft, and many others had just broken into the "smart device" market and innovation reigned supreme and changed daily. The two biggest names at the time were Apple and Microsoft. Apple was viewed as the new kid on the block, causing some commotion and ruffling some feathers. Extremely successful in their offerings, Apple change the landscape of innovation and forced it upon their competitors like nobody had done in decades. Apple became a household name quickly, and still is to this day. Apple grew large and introduced life-changing products to the market. They rivaled Microsoft like nobody else had ever done before and stood toe-to-toe with them. The headlock Microsoft had on the industry had lasted a long time, with hardly anyone posing as a serious rival to them in the tech industry. Apple, along with other issues, had Microsoft on the ropes, begging for the round to be over. But it wasn't, because Google was right behind Apple, waiting their turn.

Balmer began his journey as Bill Gates' assistant in 1980, then worked his way up to CEO in 2000. When he took over as CEO, the company was in a tough spot. Multiple lawsuits, including one from the US government, had the company tied up in legal trouble. The competition pressure from Apple and Google had the company on its heels, while the lawsuits continued to stack up. Innovation was not a priority and the complacency Microsoft had experienced was kicking them square in the ass. Apple and Google had made significant strides and grew as companies, ready to dethrone Microsoft as the top dog.

Balmer's tenure as CEO was full of excitement and drama. It was a troublesome time as the dot-com crash just happened and Microsoft desperately wanted to catch Google in the search industry and Apple in the mobile device industry. The company itself had significant product development, including a tablet. But Balmer killed the tablet development as it required modification to the Windows software package. Despite attempts to convince him otherwise, he viewed mobile software as a threat to their flagship product. What he failed to realize, and understand fully, was that innovation is about future endeavors, not current ones. Instead of expanding the flagship product and introducing a mobile version, he was finite in his thinking and killed the idea. They were essentially first to the table in the mobile software industry, but last to eat because they didn't prioritize innovation. Eventually products like the iPad replaced part of the desktop computer and laptop market share.

Not all was bad for Balmer while he was in charge. He heavily backed the development of the Xbox, and despite tough financial times in the beginning, he never wavered. The Xbox was a solid asset for the company and is still in production today. Imagine what could have been for Microsoft if Balmer would have supported their tablet and mobile software endeavors? We might all still be using Windows-based products instead of swarming to Apple or other devices.

Balmer oversaw record revenues, especially in 2013. During the first quarter alone, Microsoft's revenue hit $18.53 billion. Yes, billion. Despite all the success, combating the lawsuits, and a massive deal with IBM to make computer chips, his greatest mistake was not thinking forward.

Apple was in charge of the mobile device industry, and it wasn't even close. They were so in charge that companies were trying desperately to make products similar to theirs just to stay caught up, never mind trying to compete or beat Apple. Balmer knew this, and Microsoft developed their iPod killer, the Zune. For all intents and purposes, the Zune was a better product. It had better software, was more user-friendly, and had a better price point (at the time). I can confirm this, as my first mobile music device was a Zune rather than an iPod.

The Zune was great, yet it still died. It never took off because Microsoft was obsessed with beating Apple and the iPod. The entire purpose of the Zune was to beat Apple. It wasn't about adding something game-changing to people's lives... just beat Apple. Make the iPod irrelevant. It was an entire "our product is better" movement that didn't land with the consumers very well and the Zune died. Meanwhile, the iPod flourished because Apple advertised it as the next great product that people just had to have. It was sleek, sexy, and stylish. You had to have one. And that was the message that Apple sent. They portrayed added value, while Microsoft portrayed a bitter company jealous of the competitor.

They never sent the message of "the iPod is hands down better than the Zune," because Apple was *never* competing with Microsoft for this market. *Never.* That was the difference between Apple and Microsoft. Apple knew and understood that their only competition was themselves. That mentality kept them constantly in competition with their own innovation. There was nobody else. And under Balmer, Microsoft never looked forward enough to stand on their own. They just tried to survive. That mantra wasn't a long-term successful mentality. And the Zune died instead of becoming the household name in mobile music technology.

Microsoft was the self-licking ice cream cone, while Apple was focused on being the leader, providing life-changing value to people.

"Don't let WE be a hollow word."

I did an interview for a show one time called *Be a Human in Business*. The show featured four wonderful ladies, one of whom is my branding coach. During this conversation we really dug into what it's like to be a genuine person in business, and why showing your colors is very important. If your team knows you are hiding things, and they can't read you, they will question things. That. Is. Bad. Very bad. I dropped the above quote during that interview and thank God one of them took note, because I have a tendency to say outstanding things and not write them down. It's the main reason this book took so long to conceptualize. Not to toot my horn, but I've always been very good at giving advice, help, and mentorship, but I don't do a good job of capturing it. The quote "Don't let *WE* be a hollow word" was heavy at the time. I remember when I said it because all of the ladies on the show kind of took a deep breath and said, "Wow." And we talked further about how leadership is all about WE, not ME. And if your team thinks WE are about ME, then they think YOU are only worried about YOU. I knew that quote was impactful, and I'm glad one of them wrote it down so we could share it.

DO NOT be a self-licking ice cream cone. You are not in a leadership position, or a leader at all, if you exist to serve yourself. Outstanding leaders exist to serve others. Leaders understand we; bosses only understand *me*.

CHAPTER 3
EMPOWERMENT AND CONFIDENCE

HERE'S THE TRUTH...

If you aren't confident in yourself, you can't empower others to be.

"WE AS LEADERS, MANAGERS, BOSSES, and even employees think that empowerment and confidence is that slap on the back, the "good job" when significant results come in, or that great effort on an unexpected project. But we would all be wrong. What I just described above is approval, gratification, and recognition. It's not empowerment— it's false confidence.

"When the leader lacks confidence, the followers lack commitment."

— John Maxwell

Acknowledging hard work is great, but the confidence obtained from that recognition is temporary. Why? Because that confidence obtained is directly connected to a reason, a result, or an event. That confidence dwindles over time because without repeat acknowledgment or recognition it fades away. It can't stay relevant because it has no reason to. Nothing is fueling it. And therefore as a leader you MUST acknowledge your confidence in your team members for absolutely no reason at all.

The best base commander I ever had constantly told us how confident he was in us to do our jobs. He said it so often and with so much sincerity that you just knew he meant it. He trusted all of us to do our jobs, and he constantly acknowledged it. So much so that when we won big awards and received outside recognition, it almost wasn't a big deal. Because the big deal was having your boss, your top leader, already recognize it.

When he needed information, he came to the experts and treated us like experts. He didn't question things or try to act like the smartest guy in the room. He flat-out told us to go do our jobs, do them well, and represent him and the Air Force like he knew we could.

When I won my big Air Force-level civilian supervisor award all he did was shake my hand and say, "I knew it." Looked me dead in the eyes and said those three words with more sincerity than anything else I've ever heard (other than when my wife said yes to marrying me). He said nothing else. No "great job" or some lengthy speech about how exceptional I was and that he knew all along how great I was, or that this is a representation of how outstanding… blah, blah, blah. Nothing else, just acknowledgment of what he already knew, and frankly what I already felt. The award was just simply confirmation.

You'd think winning that award would have put me on cloud nine, but it was really just confirmation of what I and everyone around me already knew: our organization was doing great work. And we did great work before, during, and after that award announcement.

Leaders don't wait for the recognition to tell their people how great they are or acknowledge their hard work. They make the recognition known, and often. Those actions build trust and empower people like no other actions can. And again, like the old saying goes, "Actions speak louder than words."

> "Being a winner is more than getting a first-place trophy, it is acting like the effort was an honor, and the trophy is just a decoration."
>
> — Bryan Mosley

Let's break it down. To understand empowerment is to fully understand how to lead people, and fully understand what confidence is. You can master all the other things, but if you can't motivate people and empower them to do their job you've still got nothing.

Empowerment is the act of giving power to something or someone. You can find many unique examples of empowerment, going all the way back to the years of Jesus and the disciples. You can see it in some leaders today, especially some military leaders and in the growing tech world. Politicians are awful examples, and I highly encourage you not to use them as examples. They are, however, splendid examples of how not to be leaders, as they are self-servants instead of servant leaders, and they have all forgotten where they came from and who they work for. Leadership doesn't lie to your face.

To empower people, you must understand what makes them tick, what motivates them. Some people need to feel that their work pleases them. They need to feel as if their work is valued, worthy, and part of the bigger end result. For some, they just want to ensure they have their paycheck. It's important to them because they have bills to pay, a mother in the hospital, or debt from bad decisions that are haunting them. You might never find out real detailed reasons for their motivation, but you should know that these kinds of things exist. These things *power* people to work every day. What you need to do is use these things to help *empower* them. You empower people by giving them the tools they need to do their job, and do it not just well, but great. You need to understand frustrations and try to head them off. You need to give them training and then turn them loose. Give them the responsibility for their work. Hold them accountable and quietly demand a little more. Let them speak when invited to a meeting. One of the best things I ever did was tell managers to shut up at meetings and let their people speak, or don't invite them at all. Don't waste their time coming to a meeting to sit behind you and listen for over an hour. Tell your boss that you brought Karen to the meeting so she can speak to the department's updates. Give her the confidence to speak on it and discuss it with her beforehand. Study your people and find out what works but try some of these things along the way. It will make your job as a leader and manager much easier.

Now let's be very clear and honest: not everyone will respond to being empowered. Not everyone will be empowered easily, and some people just like being average, upset, and depressed. Those people will not respond to your typical empowerment strategies. These folks are going to need more and more creative ways of breaking that barrier that holds them back. It might not be something you can do, so if you feel resistance, don't force it too much. Try to push a little harder than you normally would, get creative, and try some new things. If it doesn't work, stop. You don't want to push them farther down the hole. People who are depressed, upset, or just plain unhappy have a higher likelihood of digging themselves deeper when an outside source is pushing them in that direction. So, as a leader, regardless of the level of leadership, don't push too hard when you see this.

I want to encourage you to remember that happiness and productivity can be addictive. It can attract people without even trying. So if you have people who you are trying to lead who just aren't responding, try not pushing too hard and instead letting the environment do the work for you. This is essentially what peer pressure is all about. Focus on the people around that person or persons and make the fun addictive. They might turn their nose up at it, but eventually they will have to come around. In my experiences, I've seen some very negative people eventually come around because they just couldn't resist.

I set up a potluck one time with the theme of a chili cook-off. The idea was to bring everyone together and share their chili recipes. Everyone was excited except for one person. He was a grump and hated just about everyone. Everyone in the work center knew it and they just kind of left him alone. He was a few years from retirement, and just wanted to do the bare minimum and go home. Don't talk to me, don't bother me, don't critique my work. Almost borderline disrespectful to me sometimes. And I was his boss, his leader, his manager.

I could have ignored him, allowing him to stay in his hole and be grumpy by himself. It would have been easier, and he wouldn't have infected everyone else with his grumpy mood. So, I begged him to make some chili and take part. I told him I knew as long as he'd been around that he had to have a good chili recipe in that bald head of his. I didn't know that for sure. I frankly had no clue, but I stroked his ego a little. He eventually told me that if I would leave him alone, then he would make some chili. I agreed, walked away, and didn't say another word.

Not only did he make chili, but he won the chili cook-off by a landslide. I pulled him to the side after the lunch and told him I'm glad he took part that day. Normally he doesn't. Normally he is a grump. He was wonderful at that luncheon. He cracked jokes, laughed with his coworkers, and even opened up to people. It was wonderful. I told him he normally looks grumpy and non-approachable, but he has so much to offer. I encouraged him to be more of himself here and to just be approachable. I told him he didn't need to shake hands and kiss babies like a politician, but to just be more friendly. Not to change a thing about what he did every day, but just smile more often. And I didn't ask for anything more. It took a while, but he eventually was a little more enjoyable. He was a tough egg to crack, but he was also empowered by the surrounding people. People started interacting with him differently, and he found it harder and harder to keep up with the tough guy, grumpy asshole vibe.

Naturally, as humans we want to be nice. There are just not many people who are naturally assholes. I mean, they exist, but there aren't millions of them. It's a little less common because again, as humans, we naturally want to be nice and avoid conflict. Again, there are some that don't, but we are talking about a smaller percentage. You actually have to try harder to be an asshole than you do to naturally be nice. It literally takes more effort, which is probably why people are grumps. They are so tired from working so hard on being unhappy that they are grumpy all the time and need a nap. Empowering these people can be tough, but work on the people around them if you realize this and see how the peer pressure works. If they choose to stay grumpy, fine. Let them. But empower the people around them so that their attitude doesn't ruin everyone else's.

You can't put a dollar value on a lot of things in leadership, and empowerment is one of those things. But I can tell you this: from all the people I've talked to and personal experiences, empowerment is very valuable. It can make or break your business, it can kill or uplift your culture, and it can solve a lot of problems or create new ones. Don't think that you can just give direction to people, and it will be all good. That's assuming, which is the enemy of empowerment. If your people don't feel empowered—like you have their back, that you are there to support them—they will be afraid to succeed. Failure will be their friend, and they will welcome it because they feel like it's the only option.

The littlest things you do can lead to empowerment. The confidence you show in your team, how you support them, how you react to bad news. All of it plays a part in their confidence, and therefore, how they feel empowered. As a leader, you can't walk quietly. You are the one person who others look to for stability, guidance, and consistency. So walk with authority, confidence, and determination. Your actions will, over time, influence your team members and subordinates to do the same. We are servant leaders, so we have to lead and be the example. Those examples will influence others, and they will also walk the walk.

> "Confidence is not, 'They will like me'. Confidence instead is, 'I'll be fine if they don't.'"
>
> — *Christina Grimmie*

CHAPTER 4
DECISIONS

HERE'S THE TRUTH...

You will never be more ready to decide than you are right now.

IN THE LAST CHAPTER, we talked about confidence and empowerment. The confidence you convey in your leadership and in your daily actions will influence others. It will also influence not only your decision making, but the decisions of others. Your acts of leadership and confidence could be the determining factor when someone is debating on presenting you with a good idea or keeping it to themselves. How you act when you walk in, how transparent you are, and how you act says a lot, speaking no words at all. Those things are all decisions other people make when they view you as a leader.

Decision making is a very dynamic concept. It has so many influencers and actors and can be made as individuals or as a team, or as an individual empowered by a team, or on behalf of a team. Figuring it out is almost confusing. But decisions can also be made by others because of the actions or decisions from leadership, so as I stated before, walk with confidence.

MAKING YOUR OWN DECISIONS

Making bold decisions as a leader or the person in charge is not the easiest thing to learn. There is plenty of opportunity to second-guess yourself, and even more opportunity to be wrong. The problem we have as leaders is that we think about those things way too much when we should instead be focused on making moral decisions with the information we have, free from fear. Fear of being wrong scares every one of us, even the super-rich. The super-rich didn't get super rich by throwing all caution to the wind and gambling the entire house. No, they measured the risk and made informed decisions. When you invest wisely, even with some risk associated, you can still win, and win big. And of course nobody wins without losing at first.

All right, here's the truth: waiting for more information to make decisions is always a bad idea. You will never have more information to make a decision than you do right now. So waiting for more information is only going to lead to smaller-minded and error-prone decision making.

Hesitation is a big red arrow pointed directly at confidence. So is second-guessing or holding out for more info. I'm a firm believer that the only time you wait out for more info is when you either clearly don't have enough to even decide in the first place or the info you currently have would only lead to a poor decision. Both avenues are clear, or at least they should be.

This doesn't mean that every single decision should be made quickly, but it shouldn't be drug out either. Nothing screams that I either 1) don't know what I'm doing, or 2) don't want to decide, like spending ridiculous amounts of time deciding. If you are presented with the information, and you have the facts, take the time to analyze it, ask questions, and then propose a decision. Even as the guy in charge, your decisions are still team decisions. You propose what you think the decision should be, ask for feedback and opinions, and if the consensus agrees then you've clearly made a good decision. And for a bonus, you've also gotten the team to support the decision by proposing it to them ahead of time and allowing them to think about it and express concerns, agreeable and otherwise. Never fear an honest conversation.

"Don't let your emotions get in the way of rational decision making."

— Roy T. Bennett

CHAPTER 4

MAKING TEAM DECISIONS

Indecisions only express to your team and subordinates that you are scared. And if you are scared and questioning yourself, guess what? They are going to question themselves as well! Once again, your actions have an influence.

If your actions influence them, then the decisions they make will also be influenced. Now we have an entire team of people, including their leader, questioning their decision making. The confidence level has now dropped significantly.

INFLUENCING HOW THE TEAM MAKES DECISIONS

Together as a team, you come together and decide things of all sizes and importance. But you do that *together*. That's the keyword here. Collectively, all the minds get into one room and hash it out. They analyze the info, look at the facts, and propose potential outcomes. Then they come up with decisions to make. In the military we called these COAs (Courses of Action). These COAs helped us decide and were often generated by a team all contributing their input and expertise. This process is done with you, as their leader guiding the process.

Now, there are plenty of decision made by the team that don't involve you. We made these decisions at an operational level, not the tactical or strategic level, where a lot of leaders sit.

Coworkers and team members talk to each other, as their work might overlap in their respective areas. Because of this, they often have to exchange information, discuss issues, and navigate processes together. In doing this, they will make decisions. These decisions might be minor, or they might be major decisions, but they will make them without you directly.

Indirectly, however, they could make these decisions *because* of you. As we've discussed previously, your actions or inactions have a major influence on the team. A confident leader expresses confidence out loud, both verbally and nonverbally. This affects the team members and the confidence they have. Since this seems to run downhill, that means a higher chance of excellent decisions and great conversations. The collaboration is likely to be very high and the team very cohesive.

However, when the team leader appears angry, unsure, or disorganized, guess how the team will react? It will influence their decision making, as they know the results of their decisions have consequences. These consequences will get back to the person in charge and have another consequence. If I'm a worker, and I see my boss is not in a good mood, I'm going to change my decision-making process in order to avoid a bad outcome that will only make my boss angrier or worsen his mood. Now the integrity of my decision-making process has crumbled.

That's not to say that as a leader you can't have bad days or have emotions that aren't great. Things happen at work that affect your mood for the better and for the worse. But you have to know how to get over it or use it to your advantage. If you receive good news, spread good news! It might change someone's day, and also change their outlook on their work. If you have a bad day, or get bad news, let it sink in, be open about it, and show the team that you can overcome it. It will still be bad, but the influence of the negativity will stop with you. Letting negativity get to the team will alter the team. Period. Do what you can as a leader to prevent this from happening, as the actions and decisions only funnel up to you, creating a vicious cycle.

INFLUENCING OTHERS' ABILITY TO MAKE DECISIONS

As stated previously, your actions influence the people you lead. If you are questioning yourself, they are going to question themselves. Confident leaders give their followers, subordinates, and team members confidence through actions. So if they see you sweat, guess what? They are going to sweat too.

Team decisions are different than the influence on team decisions. A team decision, as stated above, is a decision made with the collective. Your job as a leader is not to decide for the team but rather to guide them in a direction and present them with info to help them decide. The team together is a greater collective than a single person or leader. And as a leader, if you knew everything, why would you even consult the team?

Decisions are collaborative processes. Each person involved has a different perspective of the same information. A leader needs to learn how to capture these different perspectives and facilitate conversation. The aim is not for the team to make a single decision, but for the individuals to all stand by their decisions and empower the team. The problem with teamwork sometimes is that a collective team might actually decide from one person instead of as a team.

The last thing you want is one person to influence the team into making a decision that is essentially their own. Same applies to you as the leader. You can express your perspective on a decision, but because of your position, people will tend to side with you because you are their boss. Being open to other perspectives will keep your decision perspective as neutral as possible. It will take some work, but when it works, you will

CHAPTER 4

know it because people will bring new perspectives to your attention, not concerned with the possibility of disagreeing with you.

One highlight of my career was when I empowered the surrounding people to make decisions and have their own perspectives. It took time, because naturally people fear offering things and being rejected. A person's voice is their most sacred thing. When rejected it can be devastating to morale. But the more time I spent out of my office and with my people, the more fluent communication became. Ideas flowed, criticism and feedback came easier, and great ideas matured out of random conversations. Our relationship was more than just me sitting behind a desk in a swivel chair. It was more collaboration than construction. I finally hit that mark when people started to bring opinions, ideas, and new perspectives to me without fear of upsetting me with disagreement. I knew at that point that I had become an effective leader, and my team was moving with my guidance on their own terms.

"No good decision was ever made in a swivel chair."

— George S. Patton

CHAPTER 5

FALSE IDEAS

HERE'S THE TRUTH...
We believe our own bullshit, and we should stop listening to it.

MY MILITARY SERVICE was full of blunt and honest moments, advice, and guidance. Some of it was abrasive, shocking, and eye-opening. The nature of the business requires it, and instead of dwelling on it, I embraced it. It made me a better leader because I observed and studied how it was taking place. Blunt leadership, when used right, can be powerful. It's gotten some leaders in trouble because they blurred the line of power and stepped across it, thinking they couldn't be touched. They were wrong and paid dearly. The lasting effects are ones that future leaders will have to handle and frustrate themselves over, as their employees are now scarred from a previous toxic leader. It's a domino effect.

I was once told a meaningful phrase by a leader I respected. On the surface it seems blunt, maybe even rude, but it is to the point. Dig down a little deeper, and it has brilliant significance. It went something like this: stop believing your own bullshit. This means stop listening to yourself every single time you say, "Oh, it's okay," or "Oh, that will be fine," or "You are the man." Stop telling yourself that you are right. Stop trying to force your ideas to work when they clearly won't. Be humble, understanding that half of what you say, or think could be total crap. Never settle, and stop hyping yourself up. There's a big difference between self-confidence and false empowerment. Some people mistake the two and buy their own BS instead of understanding how they can still be humble while giving false confidence.

BS means you think whatever you touch turns to gold. It means you are the man, money falls from the sky, people love you because you are you. It's a privileged mentality and a false sense of success by the media, celebrities, and what you see on the internet. Twitter is your best friend, and you tweet about things you can't really take credit for. You live in a world that needs constant gratification, and you look to social media for approval. Reality is scary and you don't think you should have to work hard for hard-working results. In fact, you probably don't work hard and expect others to understand that. Well, you are wrong. So very wrong.

Confidence means that you are sure that what you touch can turn to gold with hard work, dedication, and understanding that it might not turn out exactly how you planned. You are humble, yet still knowledgeable enough to understand that you are capable of big things, but not overnight. But you are confident that with the right effort and dedication it can turn out that way. Confident in your abilities, work ethic, and determined. You educate yourself and those around you, and you seek opportunities to learn no matter what level you serve at. Humbleness is a mantra, not a word. You don't get over-confident because you have internal mechanisms that tell you to chill out and keep yourself planted on earth, unlike Mr. Twitter above who thinks he walks on water.

There is a fine line between your own BS and having confidence IN yourself. Confidence in yourself is when you know your abilities, know you are smart, and are smart enough to be humble about it. BS is when you know you are smart, and think you can take on anything, often without help. There's a big difference.

Most people need to learn this or be educated about it. I did. When I first joined the military, I was a little cocky. I was a smart and intelligent hard worker. I shortly gained favoritism with my leadership and was given additional tasks because I did them quickly with excellent outcomes. I didn't turn down work and stayed late if I had to. My family life was sacrificed at one point because I became a workaholic. Eventually all that self-gratification and praise from my leadership transformed into too much confidence and I mouthed off to a coworker one day. I mentioned I was the person who ran the show in our office. Stupid to say, but I said it and couldn't take it back. My coworker was quick to reply that she hated that about me, and it resonated. If that's how she really felt, I must

CHAPTER 5

have given her more than one opportunity to see it. She said what she said for a reason.

A few days later, I was summoned to a meeting in my chief's office. My chief at the time was a guy I really respected and looked up to. He told me a long time ago that I was an outstanding worker, a prominent leader, and was going to do great things in the Air Force. He did, however, tell me, without specifically saying it, to stop believing my own BS. He also pointed out a couple of flaws in my overall person that kept me from being truly well-rounded. It hurt. It really did. It ruined my day. But before I left, he showed me something he had on his desk. It was a small plaque with a uniform rank. It had only one stripe, usually the first stripe you receive when you join the Air Force, or upon your first promotion. It's essentially the lowest rank. He said you should never forget where you came from and pointed to that. I had already gained a few stripes but realized then that I had forgotten where I had gotten it all from. The years had blown by quickly, and I was just trying to keep up. My experiences served me well, but I forgot about remembering what was behind me, and how those things molded who I was today. The lessons learned—the growth, development, and experiences—all influenced who I was standing in front of him. Between that and his honest feedback, I really had a lot to think about.

The problem was I lacked humility. I wasn't humble about my skills, my talent, or my abilities. We had a saying for things like this. "Drinking the Kool-Aid." It meant you believed the BS, or your own truths. You believed what others told you, or you kissed a lot of ass. For me, the Kool-Aid was excellent, and I was drinking my fill for sure. I needed someone to say it to me. I needed that punch in the face.

> "When you are good at something, you'll tell everyone. When you are great at something, they'll tell you."
>
> — Walter Payton

Ever since that conversation I've always believed in telling people the truth in a manner that is always professional and helpful, not demeaning. The truth itself already can be tough to hear. Delivering it in an abrasive manner will shut the listener off almost immediately. Approaching it with a more professional delivery has a greater impact than being blunt about it. I made way more future leaders for the Air Force by doing it that way. Yes, sometimes you have to "call the baby ugly" and just tell the truth. I've had it done to me, and I've done it to others. But what happens next determines the real outcome. My policy was always simple. If I'm going to tell somebody they are wrong or doing wrong, I'm going to follow it up with why, never missing an opportunity to teach. I try not to take a lot of credit, but my approach saved a lot of careers, changed trajectory of some, and strengthened others. But it wasn't because of me; it was because of the leaders before me. Those men and women taught me the importance of stating the obvious and teaching the necessary. I owe those people a lot, and I hope they are all doing great things today (I know some of them are because I stay in touch with them). Your mind plays tricks on you to keep you from falling into a deep depression. We lie to ourselves all the time. Our brains are just set up to be self-aware. We are just wired that way. It's the emotional side to us keeping things balanced. But you must regulate it and watch it closely. The last thing you want is confidence turning into bullshit.

My dad once told me that:

"If it smells like bullshit, looks like bullshit, it's probably bullshit."

The famous East Coast hip hop star Notorious BIG once stated, "The key to staying on top of things is to treat everything like it's your first project. Like it's your first day, like, back when you were an intern."

It's that hunger and fire that made him one of the most popular rappers in history. He's considered a legend now, and he honestly wasn't in mainstream hip hop for that long, but he was wise and humble beyond his years. That kind of wisdom is incredibly valuable. You should constantly be the student and treat your peers like your professors. You don't have to look up to them necessarily, but you should let them teach you without them knowing. Be more observant than bossy. Stop believing you've got it all figured out. Be humble, be honest, and be ready for everything. Notorious BIG was hungry and treated everything he did like it was new, and never told himself how exceptional he was. He made hit music until the day he died, and if it wasn't for those unfortunate events, I'm sure he would have gone on to make a lot greater music.

All too many times we believe we know what's going on and we have a tight grip on things, when in reality we might be out of our own league and completely lost. Many people associate that with failure, which is why it's even harder to be honest and humble about it. At that point it becomes really easy to believe your own BS because you simply have nothing else to hang your hat on.

But relax and be humble. It's much easier that way and people will see it, and when they see it, they will be more enticed to lend a hand. When someone sees a person who appears full of themselves or overconfident, they tend to not bother offering assistance because it will probably come with a rejection. NEVER turn down help. You never know how valuable that help might be.

Stop believing your own bullshit and take the help offered. Once I started doing this all the time, I grew, and so did the people around me. The lessons learned served me well over the years. I finally was able to apply my knowledge, and the others around me took notice. Sometimes actions speak louder than words. I stopped believing my own bullshit and started listening with my eyes and ears. Others noticed and did the same.

Now, it often came with having to listen to duplicate conversations and advice, but everyone has their own unique perspective, so don't be so quick to dismiss it. I've learned lots of things by letting someone else just talk without interrupting them, even when I'd heard it all before. Read between the lines and listen for new clues and advice. You will NEVER get told the same thing, the same way, twice. It will never be replicated the same way. Nobody says the same thing the same way. It's all a different perspective, even of the same subject. I don't care how hard you try, or another person tries—it will never come out the same exact way twice. There are just too many human factors. Pitch, volume, sincerity, body language, etc. It simply will never be replicated the same way again. So listen up and stop believing all the bullshit in your head.

Jimmy Iovine, the co-founder of Beats Headphones and long-time leader of Interscope Records, has a personal mantra that goes like this: "It's not about you." Jimmy never sat idle. He constantly learned. He was an eternal apprentice. Jimmy has said, "I don't have a rearview mirror… just because you did something once means nothing. You have to be willing in your heart to begin again every day. The minute I'm not willing to do that, I will retire."

When he started up Beats Headphones with legendary music producer Dr. Dre, nobody thought much of it. He was one of the biggest music executives in the world, the other a legendary producer. But do you think the local electronic store or Best Buy gave a damn? Nope. They were breaking into a new market, and they had to prove themselves. Celebrities and well-known people weren't throwing their investments behind headphones. Especially high-end headphones. Not when Walmart has at least a dozen cheaper pairs to choose from. It was a start of a new thing, which meant starting from the ground up, proving themselves. Spreading the word wouldn't be hard as they both probably had thousands of connections. They probably had plenty of support with launching a new company. However, those supporters probably knew them, and knew what they were capable of. Music fans know them both for music, not electronics. Not every consumer that used headphones would know them either, so they had two sectors of people they had to try and target. Ones who knew them, and ones who didn't. Now sell them $300 headphones... they had to put in work and sell the idea. It didn't sell itself until much later on.

Ask any normal person off the street who any big record executive is, and I'd bet most won't recognize a lot of names. They will recognize plenty of artists signed to their record labels, but I doubt they recognize executives' names. Iovine co-founded Beats with Dr. Dre, a legendary music producer and rapper, but even that doesn't guarantee sales. Not everyone listens to Dr. Dre. Selling headphones to people who know you is not the biggest problem. The problem is selling them to people who don't know you, and question if your product is worth their money (the headphones are fantastic, by the way). A few years later, Beats Headphones were sold to Apple for three billion dollars. Not million. Billion. Do you think they did that by believing in their own bullshit? No, of course not. They both understood what it was going to take to get into the electronics business, let alone actually sell headphones. They jumped in headfirst, and every music artist, athlete, radio and podcast host had a pair of those headphones on their head. Social media was flooded with pictures of these headphones. It was a status symbol. Everyone wanted a pair of those headphones. Hell, I even got a pair. But they poured their hearts into that business. Both of them had been in the music business for decades, yet still had to work like they were brand new. Perfect examples of never settling, never quitting, and never letting your standards drop. You can do anything with a great work ethic and humble outlook. But telling yourself you will succeed can sometimes water down your mentality.

Same can be said for writing a book. Do you think people are just going to read your book because you wrote it? Nope. You will have plenty of people who know you and want to read it because they know you. Your family will want copies, close friends and coworkers too. But those are givens. You will almost always find success in those around you. But that's not what you are working for. You want to reach people outside your already-defined circles. For me, I wanted this book to reach leaders and managers of organizations, regardless of the industry. I have a military background, but there are far more corporate leaders than military ones. I need to reach way outside my defined circles. It will take work.

To conclude, stop believing your own BS. Take everything that you've hopefully learned throughout this book and use what you can. Never forget where you came from or who you are, and never, ever believe your own false ideas. Be humble, be smart, and be honest with yourself.

CHAPTER 5

Accept those truths, use them as motivators, and be innovative. Don't let anyone tell you that you have a ceiling or a limit. I've explored so much about myself and grew into something I never could have imagined. Do the same. Don't let false ideas about yourself draw a picture of what you look like as a leader. It's fake and only serves as a defense mechanism for support. It's not real or honest. It's how you view yourself, likely in a good light as protection. Below is maybe one of the most common quotes in history, but it couldn't be more true.

"If it sounds too good to be true, it probably is."

CHAPTER 6
Y.O.U. – YOUR OWN UNDERSTANDING

HERE'S THE TRUTH...

Knowing and understanding are two different things.

SOMETHING I ALWAYS tried to remind myself was that my brain would automatically form an opinion of something based on the probability of it harming or upsetting me. By nature we are automatically judgmental and biased. Some more than others, but by nature we as humans are judgmental. It's what happens after that initial thought that is the true perspective of the person.

My perspective on things is always a first initial reaction that I don't always agree with. It's just a reaction from my brain based on the information I just heard bounced against my historical actions and my current state of mind. It's rarely, if ever, the appropriate initial reaction. My understanding of things is biased. I can say that out loud because I know and understand it. So now when I hear things I know to take a second to digest them. I need things to marinate for a quick second before I react. Because everything that is heard has a wide range of emotions and opinions. My true perspective is a thought-out response that was given time to develop.

Leading just isn't everyone's strongest attribute. It just isn't. Some people don't even know how to lead, let alone know how to lead at their level. Others think they know how to lead at their level, but really do not know, or they have a skewed vision of how to lead. And then, some people are just poor leaders. You can tell yourself all day long that you are an excellent leader, but that's just a response developed by your brain to protect yourself. The truth might actually be that you are an average leader who needs some work. A baseline of leadership is to understand yourself, down to the grittiest truth.

YOUR OWN UNDERSTANDING

Do you understand YOU? Do you know what YOU stand for? What's important to YOU? What's important to your staff, subordinates, family, friends, coworkers? YOU is a powerful tool that many leaders just don't get. Many leaders state they understand, but they really don't. YOU has a deeper meaning, a deeper purpose. As professionals, we do often understand basic concepts, principles, and theories of many things in our field of work. But that's just a general understanding that we all SHARE. It's not really our own personal understanding because, really, we all understand the same things just a little differently.

If you step back and take a broader look, and you break it down, we all have two versions of the same understanding. One: We all understand the same concept in the same way. Like timecards. We all understand that in order to get paid we must fill out a timecard. That timecard must be signed by our boss, turned in, and processed by HR or Accounting so we can actually get paid. Most of us have a general understanding of that concept, and we can all agree on it.

Now for the second understanding. Two: We all don't really understand it the same way. For some, the timecard is a critical part of a business. We must process timecards in order to accurately depict the company's payroll expenses. If not, those expenses aren't quantified correctly and aren't an accurate example of the cost of employee labor. That also rolls over into the profit-and-loss statement, which to any CEO and CFO is a big deal because it's a snapshot of how the company performs. In the finance world you want accurate information, not information that is off. CEOs and management use this information to make business decisions, so inaccurate information is likely to lead to bad news.

Also, missing timecards turn into a nightmare for HR and Accounting. Next thing you know someone is mad because they didn't get paid. People need money in order to maintain their livelihoods, take care of their families, and put gas in their car so they can get to work. There's nothing like paying almost three dollars a gallon for gas only to show up to work and find out you didn't get paid. It will ruin someone's day.

CHAPTER 6

So, understanding Y.O.U. is important because it's your own understanding of things. Sometimes we have to listen and learn about these things in order to have a deeper understanding of them. Something as little as a missing timecard can really cause a lot of problems. As a leader, you need to understand more than just deadlines. Understand the bigger picture!

As a leader, I want the tools of the trade in order to be successful. I also want them for my people. You want me to do a job, and do it well? Train me. Don't just hand it to me and let me run with it. Train me. Invest in me. And as a leader, if you are doing the training, don't be so damn scared of someone doing such a good job that they will do it better than you. A good worker is a sign of an excellent trainer and supervisor. Do your damn job and do it well. Get yourself training as a leader and then share that with your folks. Put a priority on training your folks well and ensure it's better than how you were trained. Remember, quality is better than quantity. You aren't training to cover your own ass; you are training to make people better. Again, it's servant leadership.

Quality training will equal quality people. We just don't invest enough time in people anymore. Training, mentoring, guidance—they are all so important today, yet we spend very little time on it.

LISTEN UP! Your email to the new guy about training is not sufficient or acceptable. Written directions don't always form an acceptable form of communication, let alone training. Is it really training if it's just an email? Training tends to be more hands-on, so how does an email suffice? Carve time out of your schedule to do some training or have someone else do the training and follow up. Don't kick this under the rug; it will bite you later. I can't count how many times this has become an issue in the workplaces I've been in. It's even happened to me a few times. That's why training to me is so important. Proper training gives employees confidence, knowledge, and ownership of the job. Why would you skip, or even half-ass, this?

You've got to lead at your level and know what level that is. Some people don't know, and that's okay. Sometimes it's about discovering that level of leadership and developing it. Later on, we will talk about empowerment, which is another very important aspect of leadership. You want people to own a process? Empower them to be subject matter experts (SME). Put a priority on training and development. Make their concerns your concerns.

If you are a teammate, and not in a position of management, then the things in the above paragraphs are still things you can do to lead, and frankly, be a better teammate. Many people come to work every day, do their work, and go home. They mind their own business and just get their work done. It does not emotionally invest them in the business at all. There is nothing wrong with that. Those people aren't reading this book. You are. You want to lead or become better at leading. So, check in with your teammates from time to time. Ask them how stuff is going. If they want to talk, they will talk. Take some mental notes and try to understand how what you do in your job affects them. Because believe me, what we all do in our job's influences someone else in the organization. The minute you understand that a little better, the minute you will start seeing the bigger picture.

Sometimes leadership can be as simple as a voice. Maybe it's on a project, stepping up and taking a lead role and speaking for the group. Getting people organized and motivated to work on a project. Letting them know you are that voice that's going to speak for the group and voice their concerns and needs. Then, take that voice and actually do it. Gather info and present it to your boss. Get the team a simple win. By doing this, you can gain a lot of respect with the team, which will build confidence that when you are around, things will be all good.

YOU can't do the above by being silent. Fall back on Y.O.U. What is your understanding of it? It takes a voice to be heard. If you are going to speak up, think about what you want to say, say it to yourself, and try to hear how your peers or superiors might interpret it. Don't hear it how you say it: hear it how it will be heard by others. Then, if it still sounds good after that, speak it to the group. Use your voice to be heard, but make sure that voice has loaded words. Words that will make an impact, be heard, and encourage change. Being silent will get you absolutely nowhere.

If you get results, don't sit on them. Use that information and quickly act on it. The worst thing you could do is be satisfied with yourself and not do anything with the outcome. Take it back to the team, or the process, and implement the change. Complacency kills team momentum and progress, and only leads to laziness.

Evaluate your own understanding. Your understanding might be what's getting in the way. If you have a bad or flawed understanding, you could hinder progress for both yourself and the people you lead. Leaders aren't supposed to get in the way or be the reason progress halts. That's counterproductive. Leadership is effective, and therefore, you should be too.

Lastly, be transparent. The best leaders I ever served under talked out loud. They weren't concerned with being right or wrong but instead being open and honest. If they threw an idea out there, they expected someone to shoot bullet holes in it. They understood that process. It was their understanding that if they talked out loud, they could get different opinions and perspectives to help plan decisions and facilitate discussion. Some of the best leaders I served under were transparent leaders. They had no problem providing insight and info into their decision making. And that's tough as a military commander. There are a lot of things to consider. A lot of ways your decision affects the bigger mission.

A great leader trusts their team and subordinates, so when they speak out loud, they expect feedback. That's how outstanding leaders can come to significant decisions and move forward. Because they understand something and seek the counsel and opinions of their team. They make adjustments as necessary, and review feedback so they can make future improvements.

You, as a leader, may have your own understandings of things, but that doesn't mean you should keep them to yourself. Leadership is built around a person knowing and understanding the people around them and using their abilities to make them better. The worst thing you could do is keep your understanding of things to yourself. Every time I do that, it bites me in the ass. Every. Single. Time. It's an understanding I've learned professionally and personally.

In marriage it's a big deal. The communication in a marriage or a partnership is critical to success. If I'm thinking about how to budget our money and what repairs we need to do for our house, that's great. But what would happen if I acted on those things, deciding with the household money without talking to my spouse? What if she had ideas for a family vacation? Now we are on opposite pages. My understanding is that house stuff comes first, while she is more focused on a family vacation. Nothing wrong with either, but we aren't rich and can't do both at the same time. So, I need to express my understanding of the budget and the house priorities to her, giving her an equal opportunity to communicate the same to me. From there, we talk and formulate priorities together.

Leadership is very much the same way. We have to talk. Our understanding of things has to be transparent. It has to be shared or else we are duplicating work, miscommunicating, and causing more work. But most importantly, our understanding can't be the only thing we know. We have to listen to other things as well. Don't let your own understanding stand in your way of good actions and responsible decision making.

CHAPTER 7

VALUES

HERE'S THE TRUTH...

In order to value something, you must add value.

A TOPIC THAT LEADERS often misunderstand is value. I've seen it a hundred times. People believe that because we have put them in a position of authority or responsibility that they are valued. Or that because they are in charge, they are also valuable. That's so, so wrong. Value is not a given or assumed.

We select people for a position under a lot of circumstances. Some because it's their time to be promoted, some are tasked with responsibilities because they have handled it before and are ready for more. Others are promoted because they knew somebody who knew somebody who hooked them up. And then you have people who are selected for leadership positions because they look good on paper.

Internal hiring processes are commonplace. In fact, it's getting harder and harder to enter corporate America because of it. It's much easier to hire from within than it is to hire externally. It is a preference and isn't necessarily policy. Hell, my first job after I retired from the Air Force was almost an internal thing. I knew the work center that had the vacancy, and they knew me. It was a handshake agreement that once I was eligible to be selected, they'd hire me. Very simple. I'll be honest—I didn't value the job because I knew I would not earn it. Yes, it would have been perfect for me, and taken care of me financially. But it wasn't a job I just had to have. It was a stepping-stone-type of job. And I ended up taking another job.

My first job working back for the government was something I really wanted to do. I applied for a contracting job overseeing contracts for a distinct part of the base. It was a part I wasn't familiar with it, but the challenge of new things excited me. I was fortunate enough to land that job, and I valued it as well as the information that came with it. The opportunities I had because of that job led to other jobs, and I'm thankful for that. I really value that first government job and it holds a special place in my heart.

But value doesn't follow you everywhere. Not to that new job, the new city, or new environment. Leaders need to understand that value is limited to what value they provide. Just because you show up doesn't mean you are valuable. Value is something you have to earn. Never assume.

You can't assume value will follow you. New people, fresh faces, and new processes all don't know who you are. No matter how much someone hypes you up, there will always be skeptics and you will have to prove your value to them. Value is simply just not given out like free candy. And you should never, under any circumstances, assume it.

> "Rarely have I witnessed assumptions turn into facts."
>
> — Sonya Teclai

Value must be provided, and to provide it you must know your people as well as what you value. For leaders, this can be a time-consuming discovery, and that is why most don't even bother putting in the effort. And because of that lack of effort, things fall apart quickly.

So, let's talk about values. What are values? Values are things that are important to you. Value can be a number, like your old baseball jersey number from high school. It can be a monetary number, like the amount in your bank account you've been saving for years.

Value can also be a thing, a physical item. I have many things locked in my safe that are of high value to me. Not a resale value, as I would never part with these things. You could never offer me up enough money for some of them.

For example, I have my grandfather's flag they draped over his casket. I never met my grandfather, but he served in World War II. His military service during that war was and is still important to me, and I can't help but feel like it connected us because I also served. His flag is my connection to him, a grandparent I never got to meet. My mother says often that I look like him, something I take as an honor. His flag is invaluable to me, something I'll never part with. My entire house could burn down and if all I had left was that flag I'd be fine. I'd tuck it in my backpack and take it with me as I rebuilt.

My example above is deep-down value that you as a leader are going to have to dig for. Some people will be open about it, and others won't. That's perfectly fine, but take notice of the little things and you'll be surprised what you find out on accident.

People value things. Even the simplest of people value something. After all, if you are a professional working in a company big or small, you value the dollar, and that's why you show up daily. You can't live without it, so by default you value it. People can say they don't care about money, but to some degree every human on earth does. You can't live without it. Doesn't matter if you earn it or it's given to you. You have to have it.

The problem with value today is that nobody values it. Everybody assumes it and value dies away. Your vote counts but not when they don't count it. Value lost. Your opinion matters but not when the boss doesn't listen to it. Value lost. I prefer Lowe's over Home Depot because of an awful experience I had with Home Depot. Value lost for Home Depot. Do they care? I doubt it, but the point is you must value before receiving value.

> "There's a difference between being liked and being valued."
>
> — *Anonymous*

Values can also be things you believe in and believe passionately about. Many leaders have concepts, theories, and even quirks about them that are important. It's how they operate and how those things make them feel comfortable. That's fine because they value those things.

Experienced leaders value certain things, processes, and other things that make them feel comfortable. These are basic values that they look for. It's kind of like buying a house. There are certain things you are going to value. For instance, I'm big on maintenance. Providing me with how the seller has maintained the home is very important. It speaks volumes about the dollar value of the home. Our last home came with a three-inch binder full of information. The previous owners not only took great care of it, but they wanted the new owners to have as much history about the home as possible. It was outstanding.

I also like newer windows. Newer windows mean you took the time to upgrade something that typically costs a good chunk of money. They also help with energy efficiency, rain/water prevention, as well as privacy. Value at times does cost money, but it speaks highly at the same time.

Value works both ways. You have values and things you value, but so do your subordinates, team members, and of course the larger organization you belong to. When buying a house, my wife doesn't value maintenance and windows like I do. I tend to think of how my money is going to have to take care of the house, so the roof, windows, plumbing, and even the pavement in the driveway are all concerns. Same thing with central heat and air or a water heater. The last thing you want to do once you move in is replace a main appliance. Those are all big-ticket items. For my wife, she values more aesthetic things and functionality. If the ovens or stovetop appliances are old, she will point it out every time. Yes, they may work and function, but they are old. She doesn't like that, and to her that is important.

When we look at houses, we are looking for different things, which isn't bad, but those things have to be communicated. The values that we don't share eventually have to be shared and understood, or else we'd never decide on a house. We've bought three so far, and I think we kind of have it figured out. But it took time. I value her opinion and the things she looks for in a house. She does the same for me, because if she didn't, I'd have all the reasons to complain when I had to spend money or fix stuff! (Joking.)

"A person that does not value your time, will not value your advice."

— Orrin Woodward

Even if you're a small business, or an entrepreneur, all of those values don't necessarily correlate with each other. Bringing them all together and making them function fluidly is a massive challenge. This is especially true if you are a small business owner. What you want to do is not the same as what you need to do. Those wants versus needs will make or break a business. It's a tough decision to make, but you have to prioritize those values.

It's almost a lose-lose situation. Undervalue something that another person values, and you've lost touch with them, maybe even lost respect. Now they don't feel valued, and that could start a hurricane of negative reactions. Overvalue something and people might feel as if you are spending time on the wrong things. Lose-lose.

In the military, it was a little different. My experience was a little more cut and dry. We all valued the mission first, and other priorities second. Sometimes those second priorities were designated for us, so we didn't have to search or figure it out. But it was cut and dry at times.

For example: My job as a supervisor was always to run an operation with a dedicated mission. It was simple, and we often had a mission statement and goals provided to us. That was always my first priority, the objective I valued most. My team felt the same way, as we had embraced a "mission first" mentality. My second set of priorities, or secondary values, was always taking care of my people. This was a personal priority, as well as a priority/value the Air Force ingrained in me. The Air Force took people seriously and made it well known. I had seen my fair share of failed attempts to take care of people, and along with the Air Force, I made it my second priority and one of my largest values. If I didn't know people and know their values/priorities, how could I take care of them properly? Just throw a dart at the wall and hope I figure it out? No, that doesn't work, and I've seen too many military leaders try to do it. Let me tell you right now... you can't lead by guessing.

There are personal values as well as professional values. Understanding both will help with this part of the algorithm, as we finish up defining what EFFORT is. In order to understand values, you must put in some effort. You won't learn these things easily, as waiting for them to come to you won't work. You need to go to them, bring them out, and uncover them. In a professional workplace, you have a dynamic group of people, all with their own personalities, quirks, and desires. No, you don't need to mesh this all together and make them get along, but understanding their values will make it easier for you to help them co-exist. Expecting everyone to get along as one big happy family is ridiculous.

Professional values are things you learned in school, through your formal education, through your work experiences interacting with others, through other processes and other experts. Information you've got molded these values, people who have influenced you, and experiences you've had. Getting to know people better also means getting to know their priorities, values, and desires. Finding out these things, even if in small amounts, is critical.

Personal values are tricky, as they are values that you may have grown up with or gained over time. These are values that your environment and your culture around you have taught you. And then there are values that you have learned through schooling and interaction with other people and friends and outside influences. These values are important because this is what you bring to the table as far as culture, and who you are as a leader.

Now, the dangerous thing about personal values is that when they're brought to the workplace, they can be a sensitive subject. Not everybody is going to agree with your values, your personal values, and the understanding of it all. As a leader, remember: we can agree to disagree. Professionalism has to be maintained.

Disagreeing doesn't mean you can't work together; it means you have to listen with your ears and not with your mouth. Digest what the other person is saying to you, leave emotions out, and let it marinate for a little. Then have a discussion, find common ground, and agree to press forward. The problem with society today is that outside sources have conditioned us to think that if we disagree, we must be on separate sides. I largely blame politics, as it is a red or blue thing. Their primary argument is that the other side is bad, and they lean on that for influence. It's lazy, and frankly petty. It's created enemies and bad feelings, and trust me, that will never work in the workplace.

HARD LESSONS IN VALUE

As a leader, you have to know about these values and how they can help and hurt a workplace, and you have to have a balance of those, and a way to do that is to encourage open communication, encourage people to talk amongst each other about things. Don't make it mandatory. You don't have to tell them to talk about their personal life. None of that is mandatory, but the better people open up and are comfortable talking with each other, the easier their values will be shared and reciprocated, even if they disagree. So values are important.

Understanding value is even more important. It's extremely important that you understand your value, as well as your staff's value, because nobody wants to feel undervalued and as a leader, you can make somebody feel undervalued very, very easily. It does not take much nowadays to make somebody feel like they're not appreciated. Go out of your way to understand and recognize their value.

I know you've heard someone say, "If they don't value you, then just leave." Well, that's true but also easier said than done. I've been in a job before where they didn't value me. It was tough, as I wanted to contribute to the team at a high level, but they wanted me to fill in the gaps with work nobody else wanted to do. So they handed me the leftovers, and the programs that didn't fall into anyone else's job descriptions. I was a fill-in, and I had never felt less valued.

That kind of feeling is horrible, and as a leader you should do your best to make sure nobody on your team ever feels that way. It won't be easy, but the effort alone will at least show people that you care, and in my experience, when you at least showed that you cared, many situations didn't turn bad when they could have.

CHAPTER 7

In the experience mentioned above, I spoke up and tried to remedy the situation. It didn't go as planned, as my concerns fell on the deaf ears of the leadership running the show. My job at this location was to be a program specialist, one who was assigned to the organization to learn and grow. That was literally my job. I was there to learn new programs, grow as a leader, and contribute at a high level. I wasn't an intern. Interns fetch coffee and do the work nobody else wants to do. That's not what I was there for. I was there to be a massive asset to the organization. And they sat me in the corner. Handed me the leftovers and told me, "Shut up and color." That's military-speak for "just do your job quietly."

They did not value me the way I felt I should be valued. They valued me as a body, someone on the team they could use for manpower. In their eyes, I was just another worker, only without a job description to define my work parameters. Anything goes, in other words. My definition of my value, and their definition of my value, wasn't even close to the same. And the largest problem? They wouldn't listen or give me the time of day.

When you are ignored, no matter what position you are in, you immediately will feel devalued. It's crushing for morale and self-confidence. As much as it crushed me and made me question my career choices, it also handed me some great opportunities. I started my doctorate. I finally got serious about writing a book. I discovered other aspiring authors and even got into writing novels. At one point I even drafted up a business plan for a podcast (and at the time of this publishing I just might have seen it through!). So, although they didn't value me and didn't help me grow and learn, I actually learned a lot and opened up new doors for myself. At the time of this writing, I was contemplating putting in my resignation, as I had a lot of different opportunities that I felt very confident about.

Now, not all situations will end like that. When someone feels devalued, they will look for chances to feel valued. And that oftentimes can mean updating their resume and using company time to find another job. None of that is good.

Another hard lesson in value is the story of Microsoft and Steve Balmer. Balmer didn't understand the value of the iPod, and it absolutely crushed Microsoft. He viewed their product, the Zune, as a superior product, one that would easily resonate with customers. Well, he was wrong. Microsoft didn't value the simplicity in the competing product; instead, they overvalued the Zune and assumed that same value would resonate with consumers, enticing them to choose Microsoft over Apple. Misunderstanding value was strike one. Assumption was strike two. It was a big mistake that led to the iPhone, iPad, and competing software that eventually took market share away from Microsoft. Today, the gold standard in mobile device software is Apple. However, it could have been Microsoft.

Balmer didn't think forward, and therefore, didn't make future leaning decisions. All because he didn't understand the value and made assumptions based off his misunderstanding.

BRING VALUE EVERY DAY

Every time you walk into the office, you need to provide value. As a leader, people look to you for information and many other things that are valuable to them. It could be guidance, teachings, even humor. Your personality could be what people value. Telling jokes could brighten their day. Your ability to be humble, hate Mondays, and joke about it could change the entire dynamic. But it has to be authentic and real, not just for show.

Value can be hard to find, but don't overlook the simplicity of it. I gained a ton of respect as a leader by being open. Transparency was key, and if I was having a bad day, I never hesitated to speak about it. I found value in letting my team know I was off my game and needed to rely on them. Because they felt empowered and valued, it was nothing for them to rise to the occasion. I didn't search for value; I let it shine on its own.

UNDERSTANDING VALUE EVERY DAY

Bring value every day at work, and then you have to get people to bring value with them to work. Value has to be a culture thing, a standard practice. And then, everybody has to *understand* that value, and actually understand what it's worth, because if they don't, it's a killer. Like I stated earlier, it's a tricky thing to navigate but once you figure out how to balance it, a team can really perform.

Your team and staff bring something to the table every single day. Because of this, it's important that you understand *their* value. You need to focus on the fact that staff value, understood or not, is important to them. The people who work for you—their job means something. The words on their resume mean something. Their credentials, reputation, and intangibles all mean something to them, and they have their own definition of their value. They say you can't put a price on experience, but I disagree. I think plenty of people have a price for their value, and it sometimes isn't a number.

Take this, for example: You currently have an open vacancy you are advertising for. The job posting contains the requirements, experience, and things that you and the company value in a future employee. You need to understand that when you're asking to hire professionals with a certain amount of experience, you're saying, "I value this position to this degree." You see those things as the gold standard, hoping to get a pool of candidates all with the same credentials or better. What candidates see is potential, and they know their worth.

Even if they are not necessarily fully qualified for that position, they might value themselves as if they are. People accept new jobs not just for a change of scenery, but for growth and promotion. They value their career, and value their potential enough to hit the "apply" button and gamble on *you*.

That's right, I said YOU. Candidates gamble on you because they already know themselves well enough to apply. Their value is known. They are confident in what they do, so they take the leap of faith and risk getting denied the opportunity to work with *you*. All of those things are certain, and what isn't certain is you. When they hit "apply," they are confident in their value, but what is unknown is yours. As a leader, you must understand the other side of the coin. Not every candidate will value the same things, and some won't come with the perfect qualifications. But are we really looking for that? Perfection is impossible. What we should look for is the candidate's values, professionalism, and the ability to work as a team.

But value isn't always going to be so easy to see. Understand that their value is going to differ from how you see their value. So, you have to take a walk in their shoes; envision things through their eyes. And the best way to do that is open communication and recurring chats. I learned more than I ever would have the traditional way by just having random chats with my staff. I made it a point to rarely close my office door unless I had to buckle down on something. It sometimes put me behind, but I'd rather be behind than have a team full of people behind because they can't talk. Leaders should understand the value in that.

PROCESS VALUE

Processes are one of the single most important things in a work center. Leaders don't always interact with the same processes as their team members or subordinates, but they are still equally important. In fact, broken processes can derail the flow of a team in the blink of an eye and a leader might not even realize it. Listening when people speak, even if it doesn't really affect you, is an incredibly important aspect of any leader.

Processes are also task-specific, and as some processes are directly linked to others, changing one means you have to change another. There is a lot of value in that sentence, as change is a big deal. I've seen plenty of leaders enter a work center and immediately suggest changes to a process, not realizing how big that change actually is. For them it was an immediate fix because they didn't like it. The staff sees it differently, and now instead of change, it is a negative interruption. Now a domino effect of issues has been created that started an avalanche of problems. All to change something for no reason at all.

If you want to change something, value the opinions of the people it directly affects. Ask their opinion of it and explain why you see an opportunity for change. They might just provide some answers that would change your thoughts or provide substantial evidence why it shouldn't be changed in the first place.

Value is not only skin deep. In fact, it's down deep where you find the most value. Value is an investment and should be treated as such. You will not find value in ignoring value.

> "The most important thing in communication is
> to hear what isn't being said."

PART 2
PROCESS

Effort + <u>PROCESS</u> = Progress

The second part of the algorithm is PROCESS. Process as defined by Webster's dictionary is:

process (noun)
1. Progress, advance, something going on
2. A natural phenomenon marked by gradual changes that lead toward a particular result
3. A series of actions or operations conducing to an end; a continuous operation or treatment

I think something we've all heard is "trust the process." It's a very typical saying and I've heard it my fair share in my career and business dealings. However, it can be very hard to trust a process when the process is unknown. The quote below is something I've leaned on when I've been in those situations:

> "Hold the vision, drop the excuses, remember your why. Swerve around obstacles and trust the process."
>
> — *Karen Salmansohn*

The trust in the process isn't necessarily the process itself, but in remembering your vision/mission and dropping the excuses. As leaders, we have to do the hard things, trust the unknowns, and lead by example. You know what separates a leader from a manager? Excuses.

So drop them right now.

In this section we are going to discuss the process and your newfound understanding of effort within your leadership. How does a process work with effort, and what does it have to do with your leadership?

Well, that's simple… your effort determines how effective these processes are. In the computer world, a process only works with the right input added. Without the input, the process fails as it never even got off the ground. Input the wrong things, or half-assed effort, and you get either a failed process or a below-average result. And we aren't about below-average leadership. Save that nonsense for the politicians in DC.

The process we are specifically talking about here is how you conduct your leadership. The smallest things have the largest effects sometimes, so what are your daily habits? How are you deliberately developing yourself and others? What is your approach to development, education, and communication? Do you know how to coach? What is a mentor? Have your process down. Have it ready. You should have your strategy down so well that nobody even notices what you're doing until it's already done.

The best supervisor I ever had was always several steps ahead of me. I think I probably learned more from them than any other supervisor, simply because each step of the way was deliberate, even if I had to struggle through it. There were plenty of times that this supervisor could have pulled me up or bailed me out, but they watched me struggle. Why? Because sometimes we learn more from the struggle than we do from the lesson.

In this section I want you to gain a deeper understanding of your leadership and how it works as a process within the organization and your team, as well as trusting the process. Practice is critical because it gives experience to your strategy and processes. Don't be afraid to fail, and have some fun with it. And like Michael Scott from the office says:

"I'm always a step ahead, like a carpenter, who builds stairs."
— *Michael Scott (fictional character from "The Office")*

CHAPTER 8

DAILY HABITS

HERE'S THE TRUTH...

Leadership should be a habit, not a chore.

DAILY HABITS ARE ESSENTIAL.

We live and die by habitual functions. Habits are part of our daily behaviors and routines. Daily habits are what keep us grounded, what keep us in a solid mental state. We rely on daily habits because they are consistencies in life and work. They are things that rarely change, and things you can do without thinking. In the busy world we live in, doing things without thinking is almost refreshing.

Habits are really important, and what we're going to talk about in this chapter are two different types of daily habits. With little time left in our days anymore, and the massive amount of time we spend on our devices, habits of efficiency will help you be, think, and do better.

There is no shortage of daily habit recommendations. Upon a Google search I found at least a dozen websites offering anything from 10 daily habits to better improve your life, all the way up to 203 "must-know" habits. It's almost like a habit of recommendation overload. What I focus on, especially in this part of the algorithm (PROCESS), is how my personal and professional habits intertwine and work together, and hopefully not against each other. I never want things I do at home to interfere with my performance at work, and vice versa. It's easier said than done, but with a little strategy you can work it out to be optimal.

> "Habits are not a finish line to be crossed, they are a lifestyle to be lived."
>
> — James Clear

PERSONAL HABITS

What stands in the way between you and your goals is you. Your mindset, habits, actions, and attitude all play a critical role in achieving those goals. When life gets in the way, we often let it kick us down. That podcast you wanted to develop takes a backseat because it will be too much work. That book you wanted to write or read is shelved, as it takes precious time away from other things in life. But goals, like basic habits, must become habits. The key to hitting your goals is consistently working at them, and habits just so happen to be a consistent thing.

When I first started writing, I struggled to find time to work on my book ideas. I usually just dropped what I was doing when I felt a dose of inspiration and worked for a few hours. Those few hours might only happen once or twice a week, as life distracted me the rest of the time. I had a meeting with a gentleman named Don Staly, a book coach. He spoke with me for like an hour, explaining how he wrote his books. It all boiled down to one thing… habits.

Don wrote daily. Every day he wrote at least 2,000 words. At that rate, over twenty working days a month (average), he could write 40,000 words a month. Most professional books are between 50,000 and 90,000 words. In less than two months he could write an entire book, self-edit it, and have it ready to be professionally edited. A novel would take longer, as those are well over one hundred thousand words, but at the same rate you could still knock out even a novel in a few months. That's pretty good. But if you skipped a day, you lost a good chunk of words.

The point wasn't to force-write a book, but to make writing a habit. Then you made time for it in your schedule, and it became part of your daily life. Once I started doing this habit, waking up at about five a.m. every day, I made tremendous progress on my book ideas. I turned daily habits into a daily process, which eventually turned into progress. Many people have said the below quote, in some form, and it holds very true.

> "To take care of self, is to take care of others."

CHAPTER 8

Daily habits will also help keep you grounded, providing a sense of consistency in your life. Everybody wants to stay on the straight and narrow, leaving drama and chaos behind them. I write daily most of the time. I also read. Those things keep me grounded and provide a sense of personal fulfillment. It doesn't matter what it is, but doing it daily injects at least one good thing into your life that is strictly for your benefit only. That act alone will pay personal dividends later down the road.

As a leader, you might often find yourself doing tons of things for others, and rarely doing much for yourself. It happens. Part of being a leader is about doing things for others, but you have to take care of yourself in order to do that. So a daily habit to really get into is to do something for yourself—read, write, whatever it may be. Read a novel, read a nonfiction book, read the newspaper, or whatever you're into because it will pay benefits for not only you but for others later down the road.

A habit I formed that blends my life to my work was syncing calendars. Since I work for the government, I can't really share my work calendar with my personal calendar. Because of security reasons on the government networks, you can't hook up a personal device and use features like calendar sharing. It was a limitation that caused some headaches for no reason, so I eventually made a personal calendar through Google and shared it with my wife. From there we could both add things to the calendar and see what was going on in the Clark household.

Now that I've got two calendars, trying to balance the personal life of myself and several other people, as well as a work calendar that also includes the activities of several other people and departments, I have to make sense of it all. What I did was a weekly and even daily sync. On Sunday nights, I looked over my personal schedule for the week. Then on Monday morning I bounced that personal calendar up with what my work schedule looked like. If there were conflicts, I worked them out; if there was free time, I made a note; and if there were important things to be done, I prioritized them. From there I made a list of all the things I needed to get done that week, personal and professional. Just by doing this habit I got my life more organized and removed a bit of stress. It became a habit I looked forward to, and when I got busy, I started doing it daily. It was better to take ten minutes out of my day to sync calendars and prioritize than it was to fumble through the week, missing meetings, or double-booking myself. I drew the line when I missed an important event at my daughter's school.

Doing something for yourself is not just the only daily habit in your personal life. No, there will be plenty of other habits that will occur. Some will occur because you want them to, others because they have to.

But efficient habits will take care of the other aspects of your life that you don't see but need.

For example, sleep and stretching every morning. If you wake up and go to work with a stiff and tired body, you are more than likely going to be slow for a good part of the day. I try to turn off my mobile devices and TV around two hours before I go to sleep. After reading about how much time we spend on devices, and how it conditions us to use those devices to entertain us, I cut the time spent with them. As a result, I'm less visually stimulated later at night, and my brain can start to slow down and relax. That, in theory, should equal better sleep.

Upon waking up, I stretch. I'm not very good at it, but it gets the body moving. Yoga is the recommended thing to do every morning, as it's an excellent combination of stretching as well as a physical workout, but if you've ever met me you'd know I'm not a yoga guy. However, I have incorporated some small yoga stretching techniques, which have really helped with my bad back and sore knees. That alone makes me feel better about being active at work, as I am not a desk person. I prefer to be up and around mingling with my coworkers or subordinates.

There are tons of other daily habits you can incorporate into your life, from self-care and self-health to just basic entertainment and enjoyment. They should be part of your life, as life shouldn't be all about business all the time. These little things will lend character to your credibility.

PROFESSIONAL HABITS

Syncing up my calendars was a personal and professional habit that really got me organized so I could stay focused. I'm a schedule type of guy, so the better I plan, the better I perform. That's just me. It might not be for you, but it works for folks like me.

Daily professional habits are important to keep you grounded at work. It can be anything from a morning huddle with your team, to a daily decluttering of your desk. Whatever works for you, works for you.

Something I like to do is read leadership or business blogs and forums to find something interesting or to build my skills. I often found things I could use in the workplace, or even suggest to my team. It was value-added, and often incited creativity. When I was the chief of marketing, I did this often. When I saw new ways to advertise and market, I'd share with my team. It worked well because we started discussing new ideas more often, something that was lacking in that marketing department.

I also have an app on my phone that gives me news according to my preferences, and another app that delivers quotes. That small dose of inspiration goes a long way.

CHAPTER 8

A favorite habit of mine is being seen in the work center. All too often leaders and managers find themselves camped out in their offices for a majority of the day, forgetting that people work for them. A long time ago I started a habit of doing a walk around within an hour of arriving at work. I did Most days I could pull this off, with some days starting off busy and not affording the time. But, as often as I could, I tried to walk around and see my people. Even if all I delivered was a "Good morning" or a few high-fives, it mattered to me, and I believe it mattered to others.

As a leader, you can't be expected to remember everything about everybody. I will not remember if Rebecca from accounting saw her mother this weekend. However, I can remember to ask about her mother. There were times when I just had to write things down. I had a great office manager at one point, and she would remind me of little things like that. I made it a point to try to be personal when interacting with my team. Why? Because if I showed them it mattered to me, the things that mattered to them felt that much more important. I've never gone to one of my subordinate's kids' soccer games, but on Monday morning I just might ask about the score. Why? Because it's important to them, and when I ask and act like I give a damn, they feel important. And that action alone changes the dynamic in the office.

You also show your personal side, and it lets your team know you are an actual person, not just a suit-wearing man in charge. You actually show that you care about them and how they are doing. It's important. It was a daily habit that changed the way I led. People felt more comfortable coming to me about things, asking questions, and even delivering bad news. They felt more comfortable interacting amongst each other because they knew talking was okay. Your work center shouldn't be like the movies where the fat boss walks around in his suit and makes sure everybody works every single minute of the day. Contrary to what the movies show you, water cooler talk is okay. In fact, it's encouraged.

TEAM HABITS

Now, another thing that you should do as a leader is have some leadership type of habits, and these habits are going to be almost strictly for other people. And the purpose of having leadership habits is to build the bridge between you as the leader and the people who you serve.

"In any team sport, the best teams have consistency and chemistry."

— Roger Staubach

I had a great mentor who helped me as a junior leader tell me, "Never be afraid of a cold beer." I didn't understand what he was talking about until I saw it in person.

After a long week he took out a six-pack of beers from the office fridge on a Friday afternoon about an hour before we called it a day and ran headfirst into the weekend. He gathered everyone around and asked if anybody (of legal age) wanted a beer. And we sat around for nearly an hour and did absolutely nothing work-related at all. We laughed, we joked, and we talked about random stuff. And you know what that did? It drove morale through the roof for only $8.99.

It was a wonderful habit that everybody embraced. I forced no one to drink, but people started bringing their own drink of choice. We even had a calendar for Friday snacks, which then turned into a monthly luncheon. Nothing work-related at all, but we were doing it at work. The cohesion in the work center changed, and so did the morale. We became a team that could rely on each other, work together, and communicate better. All over a beer.

People at work are your family, like it or not. You spend just as much time with them, maybe more, than you do with your own family. Just like with your family at home, you will get along, fight, and agree to disagree sometimes. But you have to have some kind of connection in order to do those things successfully. Now I'm not saying go out there and start a minibar in your local workplace, but what I'm saying is don't be afraid of doing something similar.

Never be afraid of what an off-the-wall type of idea might do for your organization or for your team. Find habits that pay large dividends for little effort. It doesn't matter if it's a beer on Friday afternoon, or a weekly team breakfast. If weekly is too often, try monthly. But find something you all can gather around and enjoy together.

Habits are much more diverse and intense than what I've discussed so far. But the important takeaway is understanding how habits affect our lives, and the lives of others. Habits may be little things, but little things can become big things, and big things take big efforts to overcome. Instead, do the little things right, and the big things won't seem so big. The below quote is another one that has been said by many people, in several different forms, but hits the nail on the head no matter who it has been interpreted by.

> "It's the little things in life that matter the most."

CHAPTER 9
DELIBERATE DEVELOPMENT

HERE'S THE TRUTH...

Most leaders don't develop their people correctly, let alone have a plan to develop them with purpose.

DELIBERATE DEVELOPMENT is a term I've heard a million times from my military experience. Essentially, it's all about finding a specific purpose to develop and grow your people, team, and organization. In this chapter, we are going to discuss development and the three different avenues of growing the team as well as yourself in leadership.

Deliberate by definition means to do something on purpose, for a reason, and for an intended outcome. Leadership needs to be deliberate and done for a reason. If you want to lead people, you must develop people.

Over my many years in the Air Force I heard the question, "What are we doing to deliberately develop our people?" It was asked repeatedly. Are we investing time, efforts, and resources into our people? Do we value them enough to create opportunities for them to learn, grow, and even lead? They are all important questions, and as we spoke about value earlier, development is an important value to both yourself as a leader and to others.

> "Development is about transforming the lives of people."
>
> — Joseph Stiglitz

Development, by definition, is the intentional teaching, learning, and absorption of information. It's how we learn. It's how we grow. You've been developing your entire life from the minute you left the womb, because when you were in the womb, you only knew how to just curl up into a ball. But the minute you left the womb, you had to learn how to do those things on your own, even if it meant, you know, opening your own eyes.

Over the years you learn to talk, as well as crawl and walk. Life is a constant act of development. So if we are constantly developing as people, why wouldn't we constantly develop as leaders at work? Leadership is about taking care of others, and development is one of those ways. We take development a step further and deliberately grow people as an act of investment. Better employees can equal a better-performing organization.

There are three areas of deliberate development that I focus on: personal development, teaching, and education. The differences among the three are critical for leaders to understand. Each area has an intended purpose in the whole-person concept. This concept is about creating and developing unique individuals who are ready to lead or to be experts in their field. Remember, we aren't developing and training people to replace us someday; we are doing so because they will be better than us someday.

PERSONAL DEVELOPMENT

Personal development is about you, personally or professionally, or maybe even both. The intent behind personal development is finding ways to do the following:

> **R.I.C.H.**
> Relax
> Increase Knowledge
> Create Opportunities
> Hear the Truth

RELAX

In our busy worlds it's often so hard to take time for ourselves, and then when we do, we are behind. It almost feels like a burden. Take a

CHAPTER 9

two-hour nap, then you are two hours behind on laundry. Add kids to the mix and you are two hours behind on EVERYTHING and, depending upon their ages, you probably have messes to clean up. Relaxing can be such a pain.

One of the biggest problems today is that professionals don't have hobbies, or if they do, they don't exercise those hobbies much. Relaxing hasn't become a priority, and there's no down time until it's time to go to sleep. That constant operations tempo is going to run you into the ground. And leaders can't perform like outstanding leaders if they are burnt out.

Take the time to learn more about your interests. If you are really wanting to step it up, join some local groups and get yourself out of the house and talking to like-minded people. Develop daily habits like reading, writing, or doing whatever it is you like to do. It's important to find time for those things.

A perfect example is larping. If you don't know what larping is, well, you better Google that. Larping stands for Live Action Role-Playing, and it's where people join together and role-play, primarily in medieval themes and games. In all honesty, people make fun of it all the time. And I have to admit, it looks goofy. However, they have got it figured out.

Instead of dropping all work-related things at five p.m. on a Friday and wasting away a weekend of drinking, eating, and being a couch potato, these guys wake up early on a Saturday, dress up, and role-play for several hours. With hundreds of people sometimes. And it turns into an event. Food, fellowship, and camaraderie. Time to exert energy outside of work. Time for self. And yes, increasing their knowledge of history is part of it. Not so goofy anymore, is it?

The amount of creativity they use to create these live-action stories and then play them out is actually pretty amazing. It's like writing a script to a movie in real time. It's a huge endeavor, and it's pretty entertaining to witness. The point here is this: What are you doing to increase your knowledge? We find knowledge in almost everything. What are you doing to increase it? Are you doing anything at all to feed the machine?

It doesn't have to be rewarding; however, it can be rewarding. But you must schedule time for it. That's right, schedule time for it. I wake up every morning around five a.m. just to do something for myself. First, I read for twenty-to-thirty minutes daily. Next, I write for at least thirty minutes a day. This helps me make progress on the multiple writing projects I'm working on. This time is for myself, as it's my only time of the day that nothing is scheduled. Finding that time is important for mental health and life balance, so don't overlook it.

Instead of trying to find time to relax, I schedule it.

INCREASE KNOWLEDGE

Take the time to increase your knowledge of subjects that are important to you. It doesn't matter if these subjects are work-related, hobby-related, or just personal interest items. They could be professional interests that help in the workplace. It could be a conference that you've wanted to attend. Take the time to read and learn more about them. You never know when they might come in handy. Plus, you will keep the mind sharp and have a sense of fulfillment.

I've always pushed my people to do this. I encourage them to find opportunities to increase their knowledge, especially in their areas of expertise.

CREATE OPPORTUNITIES

Much like Increasing Knowledge mentioned above, Creating Opportunities is about expanding your knowledge and sharing that knowledge. As humans, we often stick to the script and don't go too far outside our comfort zones. It feels safe and keeps us feeling that way and doesn't challenge us at all. For some, that's just fine. But for others it's not. Seek opportunities for and even create some of your own, but don't shy away from them.

Great ways to create opportunities are to have working groups or master classes. Master classes are cool because one person teaches about their area of expertise. You can hire people to come in and teach a master class, or even better, have an employee put one together. It taps into the creative side of things, while giving someone an opportunity to share their knowledge. Win-Win.

A big thing to remember for opportunities is that they won't always come your way. More often than not, you are going to have to make your own opportunities.

HEAR THE TRUTH

For a personal development topic, this is Beethoven's Symphony No. 5. Hearing the truth is so important.

On a personal level, you have to be able to hear your own truths. As a people, we don't necessarily shy away from truths about others. In fact, those truths really fuel the rumor mill. But telling ourselves the truth? Not as common.

Hearing the truth is just honest feedback from either yourself or your peers. Regardless, it's good info to hear. Analyze it for what it's worth and use it to your advantage. This is an opportunity for growth, and it doesn't matter if you are a leader, an aspiring leader, or a member of the team. Growth is growth. Combine it with the rest of the above and you'll be R.I.C.H.

TEACHING

The second area of development I like to focus on is teaching. Teaching is how we develop skills and skill sets. Teaching is hands-on, job-related training that is targeted to specifically grow and increase skills in the job.

Teaching is an investment. You must teach the job so your people can learn skills to do the daily work, be successful, and accomplish tasks. Just because you've hired or taken on a qualified person does not mean you can neglect this principle. Teaching often requires hands-on instruction and demonstration. The goal is to teach more and more about the daily duties, tasks, and responsibilities as a team member finds their place. Growth in the areas of efficiency, performance, and basic skills knowledge cannot come if you don't build teaching into your leadership.

Teaching is an essential first step in developing the team. Better-prepared team members will be ready to tackle larger projects, workplace issues, and personal challenges. The more you teach, the more skills the team has. The more skills the team has, the more efficient they can function.

As a leader, this burden is not solely on you. No, you don't have to stand in front of everyone in a conference room and lecture for hours at a time. That's ridiculous. But what you can do is create opportunities to teach in group settings and facilitate discussions. A good facilitator will guide the discussion, leverage other experts, and let the learning happen. A good leader understands how to facilitate, and therefore, how to really teach. Remember, you aren't the expert in everything, so why would you think you should teach everything?

Also, there are leaders within the team who can teach others, and you can rely on outside teachers and team members. You can even hire professional consultants and guest speakers. The possibilities are endless, so don't be narrow-minded. Teams can be self-sustaining objects, capable of great things if they have the tools to work with. Get creative.

EDUCATION (OR PROFESSIONAL DEVELOPMENT)

The last part of development involves education. I focus on this in my leadership because this area is where outstanding leaders can really shine and make a difference. Especially today, where we put leaders into very dynamic workplaces, leading accomplished people. That doesn't mean those leaders know everybody's job inside and out, but it means they have to connect and know them.

Now, you might ask, "What's the difference between teaching and education?" Well, I'm glad you asked. Development through education takes teaching a step further. Teaching is about growing people through work skills specific to their trade or specialty. Education is about growing people through professional development. Together they form the duo of creating well-rounded people.

There is a vital but simple difference between teaching and educating. You teach people so that they can carry out tasks correctly. You educate people so they can become expert professionals. Education is professional development and opportunities to grow outside of the skill sets and parameters of their specific job. These topics are not job- or task-specific, more so work-center-specific or discussions on professionalism. Education is a great place to teach processes like Lean Six Sigma, Project Management, and even other certifications. Not job- or task-specific, but things that grow people into more than just workers.

As leaders, we educate in order to create valuable employees and future leaders. We often call this professional development. This type of deliberate development calls for knowledge outside of the job skill sets. Instead of subject matter experts, we want team members to also become professional matter experts (PME). The focus here is to build character, leadership, and people-related knowledge in the workplace, but not related to the specific job. Leaders can educate on everything from being a team leader to lean management principles to effective communication. This education can be vast, or even specific to the organization's needs. The beauty of education is that it is limitless and can be tailored to the organization's needs.

Training and developing people are often duties that organizations overlook. We assume that because we hire people with great backgrounds, experience, and education that we are hiring plug-and-play team members. Not true.

We base the hiring on job needs and talent availability. You won't hire the perfect candidate every time, and if you are trying to find that perfect hire you will probably wait a long time. If you want four years of experience, expect to get applicants with more experience, as well as less. But does that mean because they are overqualified experience-wise that you have to *NOT* develop them?

Instead of hiring for perfection, why not hire for capability, suitability, and abilities? With those things right there, and a deliberate approach to development, I can build people that fit my mold and become game-changers. All I need is the right candidate.

CHAPTER 9

Development is still necessary in order to influence culture. A culture can go sour quickly when you aren't actively developing people to become greater humans. As a leader, take a deliberate approach to development, find your niche, and invest highly in developing the team. The aim is to grow the whole person through deliberately developing all aspects of their being and improving their lives.

> "The growth and development of people is
> the highest calling of leadership."
>
> — *Harvey S. Firestone*

CHAPTER 10
PLUS, MINUS, EQUAL

HERE'S THE TRUTH...

Preserving job security is bullshit.

THIS ISN'T GAME OF THRONES. Nobody is grooming their successors to take the Iron Throne so they can turn around and have their former leaders bend the knee. Nope. Nobody is coming for your job. You will not get fired because someone is better than you. If you are worried about that, well, I've got some bad news...

As leaders, we can't fear who might come after us. The next up-and-coming employee with huge potential is not a threat. If anything, they are an asset. But yet, so many management-level leaders fear it. And because of that, they think job security is making sure they, and only they, have all the info. The young guns can't rise if they don't know what they are doing, and therefore, they have to look to me for the information. It's what these management-level leaders call job security. I call it bullshit.

Deliberate development is simply developing people on purpose to have better skill sets, utilize their talent, and sometimes discover talent and abilities they never knew they had. It's an enormous investment, and people love to feel valued and invested in.

Development sounds like such a great idea, but the problem is that most leaders do not know how to actually do it. There is no rhyme or reason to how they approach development. And they don't know the difference between development, teaching, and education.

Previously we talked about deliberate development and how to grow the whole person. It sounds great and works out really well when done correctly. But that's most of the problem—nobody takes a good approach to development.

Death by PowerPoint is not development. It's not someone talking to you while slides click away, telling you mostly information that you've heard before. Development is not waiting to see whether someone sinks or swims while performing a hard task and then shrugging your shoulders when they fail. The phrase "You have to fail to know how to get back up," is a great quote, but it's a quote. It inspires and motivates when failure occurs, not be the basis for a development plan. Watching someone fail just so you can point it out to them, and then train them the right way—or worse, make them figure out what they did wrong—is not development. None of that is development. That's all management just trying to check the box. "We did it, we taught them things!" Wrong.

> "The growth and development of people is the highest calling of leadership."
>
> — John Maxwell

My personal philosophy for deliberate development was to create a schedule and pick topics to teach and discuss. It was just enough to check that box and make me feel like I was doing my job as a leader.

What. A. Joke.

How can you create a schedule and just expect those topics to be relevant six months from now? Businesses and organizations move and grow pretty quickly nowadays, so you really think those topics will still be applicable? What happens when a subject comes up tomorrow, but you aren't scheduled to train on it for another four months? Do you just blow it off? Or do you address it then? If you address it then, you screw up your schedule!

Scheduling specific development is a waste of time. If you want to create a schedule, then fine. Create the schedule for the simple act of getting organized. Solidify your time and place and call it good. But don't pick a topic just yet. Allow yourself some wiggle room to address the organization's needs as those needs come up. I used to think schedules worked well until I realized I was trying to check the box on completing my duties as a leader, and that mentality rubbed off on my team. They took the same approach to learning. Let's just check this box and make the boss happy. Total. Waste. Of. Time.

I started researching innovative ways to develop people, teams, and even larger organizations. I didn't want some program to download or purchase; I just wanted a concept that I could use to launch my creativity. The last thing you should do when stuck in a rut is to keep trying to climb out without help. If you are in a creative spot and stuck without ideas, reach out for help because sitting around waiting for ideas to come to you is a waste.

What I found was Ken Shamrock's philosophy on developing fighters at his coaching business. Ken Shamrock is a legendary mixed martial arts fighter, coach, and advocate. He paved the way for many fighters today and was part of mixed martial arts and ultimate fighting way before it was mainstream. His approach to growing as a fighter led him to at one point be labeled as the number one mixed martial artist in the world, and in 2008 was ranked by Inside MMA as one of the top ten greatest mixed martial arts fighters of all time. After he spent many years in the fighting world, at many levels, he moved on to professional wrestling. A wrestler by nature who picked up different forms of martial arts, Ken spent years in the professional wrestling world making the ankle-lock submission hold extremely popular. It was polarizing, and so was his career. Toward retirement from both fighting and wrestling, he founded the Lion's Den mixed martial arts training camp. He now trains fighters and prepares them for the challenges within the multiple mixed martial arts levels of professional fighting.

In fact, even he called it development, not training. Shamrock's purpose toward developing fighters was to not just teach them a fighting style and art form, but to develop those skills that they will also need inside the ring. He wanted to deliberately develop them to a championship level—fighters prepared for everything. To develop those instincts, reactions, and attributes that they would need in the ring, octagon, or venue. He obviously saw a need for the whole-person fighter concept, and employed a technique to do so called *Plus, Minus, Equal*.

We can use this technique on deliberate development in nearly any situation, in nearly any organization. As a leader, this technique is essential to not only develop your team, but to understand them as well. If you walked into a business today, I'd be willing to bet that eight out of ten owners/managers/leaders could tell you right off the bat who their top employee was. But does that title mean we stop investing in them?

Stop developing that top employee? No, it sure doesn't. Learning should never stop, and we should never reserve it for only the top.

So Shamrock used the *Plus, Minus, Equal* technique like this:

PLUS:
The fighter I paired you with is better than you. You not only have a lot to learn, but you must rise to the challenge. You risk getting run over and trampled. It brings out the best in you and makes you rise up.

MINUS:
The fighter I paired you with is not nearly as good as you. Being patient is key, because your elevation in skills could get you or the other fighter hurt. Focus in this pairing is on teaching, patience, and understanding. When you are in the ring, your opponent is out to beat you and is bett ctly what, but you know it exists. Patience, teaching, understanding.

EQUAL:
The fighter I paired you up with is equal to you. Interacting with them is like looking in the mirror, seeing the reflection. They can copy your moves, predict your next move, and counter your moves. This is the ultimate chess game. Using the aspect of Plus and Minus, combined with the understanding of the person across from you, means being equal takes skill, knowledge, and persistence.

Obviously in the workplace we aren't developing fighters, but we are developing talented team members and growing the whole person. So the *Plus, Minus, Equal* technique can work quite well as it's not a combat-related concept, but a concept everyone can embrace. It's a concept that should be used as another tool in deliberate development, a topic we've spoken about previously.

In its essence, the concept uses the best students to help train the ones who need the most work, and to train the best students on how to be patient when they are on top of their game. In order to stay on top, you have to preserve when a challenger approaches. How do you think so many big entrepreneurs became worth millions and even billions? They rose to the top, and once on top, focused on staying on top. Patient on the way up, patient while on top, and always learning.

CHAPTER 10

Speaking of challenges, the *Plus, Minus, Equal* concept is really about learning to be challenged. Being challenged is a part of development that is very often overlooked and not acknowledged. Challenges force us to do one of two things: 1) rise to the occasion, or 2) quit. This concept requires you to rise to the challenge every time, no matter if you are the better fighter, the lesser fighter, or just as equal to the guy (or gal) standing across from you.

"Companies don't give job security. Only satisfied customers do."
— Jack Welch

CHAPTER 11
COACHING AND MENTORING

HERE'S THE TRUTH...

Coaching and mentoring is not about being in charge; it's about opportunity.

COACHING AND MENTORING can be tough work. It's a variable dynamic between not just leader and follower, but also between peers and different subject matter experts. Many people coach other people. We often assume that in order to coach, you have to be in charge. Not true. Same goes for mentoring. You don't have to be in charge to do any of these things. In fact, you can be just about anybody.

In over fifteen years of government service, and another six in the private sector, I realized that I was often not the smartest person in the room. However, I knew how to share information. I've worked many jobs where I was not the most qualified, not the most knowledgeable, and not the highest-ranking or highest-paid. But in most places I've also been the guy everyone looks to for answers, solutions, or a way forward. I was a leader among peers, and also to my bosses. I've had plenty of superiors come to me for help, guidance, and understanding. It's not about being in charge; it's about knowing how to take charge when given the opportunity, balancing your knowledge and abilities with the knowledge and abilities of others around you. I've lived off the below quote. It's been repeated a million times throughout history, and I've used it probably about the same number of times. It rings true and has so many applications.

"You can lead a horse to water, but you can't make him drink."

When an opportunity arises, there is something you must understand. You can *lead* a horse to water, but you can't make him drink. The problem many leaders have is that they get opportunities to give out advice, coach someone, or mentor others, and they get upset when that person doesn't listen to them. Understand this: coaching and mentoring is meant to expand someone's understanding by gathering expert opinions and useful information. That doesn't mean it will be used. Coaching and mentoring are not direction and guidance. The best coaches and mentors give advice, opinions, and useful knowledge and then let the person being coached or mentored run with it. So, if those being coached or mentored don't listen to you, understand that wasn't their plan in the first place. I've been mentored, coached, and guided by many people in my career. I've listened to and ignored all of them at various points. Why? Because I seek their counsel and take what I need from their words. That's the entire point. Their perspective gives you things to think about that you might not have.

If I want direction, I'll ask for direction. If I need what we call a vector check, which is the boss's thoughts on an issue or topic, I'll ask for it. Need new courses of action (COAs)? I'll ask for them. It's as simple as that. Information that is direct and to the point. It's supposed to be black and white. Simple, direct, and usually without question. No emotions involved.

For many leaders this is tough, especially passionate leaders. Understanding that people will often ask for your advice, and then not listen to you. You ever think that's because maybe they sought out multiple opinions or counsel from multiple people? Maybe they heard something better than what you said, and their gut told them to go with that. If so, be happy if they succeed, and be there for them when they fail. It's all learning. You can't protect people all the time. Let them fail a time or two. The best lessons are often found in failure.

The problem is that *you* want to see the person who you mentor or coach do well, especially with the advice you gave them. But those feelings come from a selfish place, a place of self-gratification, whether you like it or not. You are happy for them because you helped them. Do you feel the same when they do something without you? No. No, you don't. Because your emotional factors come into play, and you have a direct, vested interest. Cutting ties with that emotional investment is

CHAPTER 11

a must when you are coaching or mentoring, because people will not always do exactly what you say. But that's the beauty of coaching and mentoring. You can provide honest, direct, and sometimes even unconventional advice to the listener, knowing they will take from it what they want, and since you have no ownership interest, you don't necessarily have to be successful. If they are successful, then great. If they fail, well your job is to be right there to pick them up and coach/mentor them again. But fear of failure teaches nothing.

Now, there are several types of people we coach and mentor. On one hand, you have people who want to be coached, mentored, and groomed. They desire to be great at their job and can take criticism, constructive feedback, and sometimes even denial well. They look at it as learning opportunities, or opportunities to grow. You can lead these folks to water and know they will drink it. If they don't drink it, they can then listen to why it's important to drink the water. It's hard to knock them down and they are rarely deflated or defeated. They can take the punch right on the chin and recover over time. They have their eyes on the prize, or on an end goal. Everything can be a teaching/coaching opportunity if you let it. You also have people who want to be mentored and coached, but don't want to hear the truth. They want you to tell them what they want to hear. You will disappoint them every time, because your job as a leader is not to protect and babysit them all the time. This the hard part of leadership that so many fail at because they are scared of the consequences. Again, you have no ownership interest, so give them the real deal. Don't hold back. You owe it to them to give them the info they *need* to hear, not the info they *want* to hear. Polite and professional honesty are invaluable tools when coaching and mentoring people.

And then you have people who don't want to be coached and mentored. They don't think they need it and assume they can figure things out. They think coaching and mentoring are like directions and guidance, and just like some leaders, they have the wrong outlook on coaching and mentoring. In these cases, their egos need to go. Even the president of the United States seeks counsel from previous presidents. If you think they don't, well, you are wrong. One could argue, perhaps, that the president doesn't even really run the country; the people around him/her do.

Coaching has really become a hot topic, with many organizations even hiring out third-party coaching companies to teach their employees how to be coached, and what to look for in a coach. Coaching has become a profession outside of sports, and that's a good thing.

A mentor of mine once told me, "To be a coach you must be coached." I thought it was kind of dumb because I wasn't being coached at the time (in my opinion), but in reality, he was coaching me daily. He was giving me info and guidance that I could use and letting me talk out loud with him. I was energetic, and he didn't stop me from taking on projects. Instead, he let me run and empowered me with knowledge and tools to do those jobs. I didn't realize it, but by capitalizing on the free energy I had, he was building me up. He didn't always talk a lot. Sometimes he just listened and let me talk out loud. Afterwards he'd chip in corrections or things for me to think about. My mindset and talents molding right in front of me, and I *thought* I didn't need to be coached. It was genius, and something I've copied (thanks, Shane).

I've dealt with my own mixture of people who needed to be coached and mentored as well. There was no shortage of energy, and no shortage of egos and stubbornness. Egos impede smart thinking and responsible decision making. Stubbornness impedes being humble, and if you aren't humble, you can't be coached. I was once that way. A young professional thinking I could figure it all out. I was wrong.

Coaching and mentoring people who don't think they need it is a tough challenge. It's frustrating, intimidating, and awkward. Especially if the person outright doesn't want it.

Should you even bother coaching or mentoring someone who doesn't want to be coached? Yes, of course you should. If you don't, you might miss out on a great opportunity.

Historically, there have been many people who have skipped coaching or mentoring just to receive it later on. Take Kobe Bryant, for example. He skipped college to go straight to the NBA. He didn't feel the need to be coached or mentored, or even play at the collegiate level. Hard to argue with him really, as he was a pretty outstanding player from the first day, he stepped onto the court for the LA Lakers. However, that version of Kobe Bryant would have likely not achieved the level of success he eventually got without great coaching and mentoring. He went on to a twenty-year career, getting five NBA Championships and eighteen All-Star appearances. Dominating basketball for two decades is no simple feat. His impact and play molded future players and will for decades. If you look at Kobe Bryant during his first year in the NBA, compared to his last year, he was an entirely different player. Growth, coaching, and mentoring changed his game forever.

We could say the same of Michael Jordan. Unlike Bryant, Jordan went to college at the University of North Carolina. He was no doubt a special player, something the Chicago Bulls understood when they drafted him in 1984. Jordan quickly became a fan favorite even in opposing arenas. Despite how good he was, Chicago didn't win its first championship until 1991, almost seven years later. Phil Jackson, a legendary basketball coach, joined the Bulls in 1989 as a brand new coach. It took Jordan

CHAPTER 11

and Jackson, as well as a roster of upcoming stars, to take over the NBA. It was talent, combined with the willingness to be coached, that made good coaching and mentoring build a champion. Success found the Bulls twice during Jordan's era, in the form of two three-peat championships. One from 1991 to 1993, and the other from 1995 to 1998. Some would argue that if Jordan hadn't retired and played baseball during the gap, the Bulls very well could have won eight or nine championships in a row.

Coaching, mentoring, and teamwork made all of that happen. Yes, Jordan was a superstar. But he wasn't a superstar on his own. Phil Jackson orchestrated the play around him, fostering an environment where he could succeed. He did the same with the rest of the roster, fostering future household names and superstars in Scottie Pippen, Horace Grant, and even Steve Kerr. And Jordan pushed his teammates harder than anyone else did.

As a leader, don't be afraid to be coached. You don't know it all. Most importantly, you can't coach anyone if you aren't being coached.

When I ran a small part-time coaching business, I struggled to get clients. I had a few, but it was nothing big. I didn't think I needed a coach for my coaching business. However, I bit the bullet one day and hired one.

And it changed my entire business around. Not only did it give me great info, but it also guided me in a direction I needed to be successful in my business. I knew what I was talking about, and I was an excellent coach. What I wasn't good at was landing clients. I needed professional help to assist me with recruiting people who needed to be coached. And the biggest selling point I had was: I had a coach myself.

When I told people I was a personal and business coach, with my own coach, it lent a ton of credibility. It made what I told people was important about coaching actually feel relevant. They saw my success, and my purpose behind having a coach, and had no issue signing me up to be their coach. At one point I got so busy I had to turn people away!

Bottom line: coaching is not an admission of defeat or failure, but an admission by those who are smart that they need all the help they can get to achieve their goals. There's a big difference. Coaching is an important part of the leader's algorithm and purpose.

> "All coaching is, is taking a player where he can't take himself."
>
> — Bill McCartney

CHAPTER 12
CHANGE

HERE'S THE TRUTH...
Everybody hates change. Nobody can explain why.

NATURALLY, WE HATE CHANGE. Humans, by nature, are repetitive people. The idea of mastering a task and becoming efficient at it is ideal. It works for us because we can figure it out, not waste any more time, and be successful. If it works, why change it? If it ain't broke, why fix it? That's our natural mentality.

But let me tell you this... we only hate change because we've been told to hate it.

We hate change because we've been told repeatedly that change is an ugly, naughty word. Change is a bad thing because it's disruptive. We hate it because it changes our daily routine, our daily things. It's disruptive, and people don't like that. Well, here's the truth—change is supposed to be disruptive, that's why it's called... *change*. And yes, change is *good*.

Change has an unfair stereotype behind it. In the workplace it's become a naughty word. Nobody wants to change anything, especially if it works. Truth is, change is a powerful tool. Change is good. Change is a process that also needs dedicated attention so that it will be successful.

You can't expect to just make a change and for it to go over well. That just won't work. Change is and is supposed to be an entire process. That process is designed so that you can go over a lot of details, get the point of the change defined, and embrace the change. The biggest part of change is not change itself; it's selling it to the people you lead.

You can tell someone until you are blue in the face that this change you are proposing will change their lives forever, and in a good way, and they will still decline it. Again, it's because we hate change. We've become conditioned as a society to hate it. Who's to blame? I got no idea, but when you have to change politicians just as often as baby diapers, and for the same reason, people tend to tire of change. The problem with p is that they promise change, and then only provide more of the same. The promises are now just lies, and people tire of it. As a leadership rule, I always under-promised and over-delivered. If I couldn't promise it, then I said so. But I tried to never promise something I couldn't deliver on. When it comes to change, you never make promises. Failed promises will equal failed change, no matter how good it could have been.

I studied change management and Lean Six Sigma in college. At the time it wasn't as big in corporate America as it is now. The world economy hadn't hit the point where technology advances were changing people's lives for the long-term yet, but it was coming. I remember taking a college class at night in Wichita, Kansas. I was stationed at McConnell AFB and taking classes for my undergraduate degree at Southwestern College. The class was on public speaking, and it was during the presidential debates before Barack Obama was elected.

Obama was up against John McCain, a tough Republican senator from Arizona. The country was coming off of eight tough years under President Bush, reeling from the attacks of 9/11 and ongoing wars in Iraq and Afghanistan. Obama promised change, and lots of it. So did McCain, but not in the same manner. I don't care too much for politics really, but I have to admit, as a registered Republican, watching Obama speak on TV really sold me.

His charisma and character sold me on the need for change. The adopted language and manner in which he spoke talked to me directly. He connected with me, a Republican, who had intentions of probably voting Republican regardless. However, as the class sat there and watched Obama and McCain speak, I realized who I was supposed to vote for. Obama simply outspoke McCain. He was a better speaker, better presenter, and appeared as the better candidate. Obama mentioned change like it was a good thing and made this lifelong Republican convinced he would bring it.

CHAPTER 12

Barack Obama eventually became President Obama, with that same charisma that he had on TV that night. He sold the country on change, and it won him the White House. Change indeed had captured the Oval Office.

The problem with Obama, like every other politician campaigning for office, was that they promised change they couldn't deliver on. I try to stay away from intimately talking politics, and I frankly don't care if you are a Republican or Democrat. What people don't realize is that the president can't act on major policies with the stroke of a pen. Of course they can sign a ton of executive orders, but those only go so far. For actual changes to laws, Congress has to draft legislature, pass it in both chambers of Congress (House and Senate), and present it to the president, who in turn signs legislature into law. A presidential candidate can campaign for all kinds of change, make tons of promises, and even win the White House, but they can't do that alone. Executive orders expire. It's temporary change advertised as promises. And nearly every candidate does it at all levels of politics. And because of all that, *change* has become an undesired word.

Bottom line: you can't disguise change as promises. People will see right through the bullshit.

I learned a valuable lesson early in my career about making promises. I made promises because I thought that was what got people to believe in me. Then, if the promises fell short, I could apologize and try again. No harm, no foul. Sorry, I was wrong. But it doesn't work like that.

Promises are nothing if nobody believes in them. That's why when I see politicians campaigning to lower the deficit, approve whatever policy, or overturn a previously instated law, I just laugh. They over promise and almost always under deliver. If you want to learn how NOT to lead, follow politicians closely. We gripe on them as elected leaders while they break promises all the time, hence, why we gripe about them. You can't be a moral leader while breaking promises. If you had credibility and trust before, you won't have it anymore.

My lesson in making promises was simple: try not to make them. Instead, establish expectations and tell them what you are going to do. The effort is much more understood than the broken promise. If you come through and get something amazing done, people will be happy and maybe surprised at the outcome. But the feeling of letdown will strike every time a promise is broken, no matter how big or small the promise is.

The below quote has been used many times, by many people. Its applications are vast, and in its simplest form it maybe makes more sense than anything else I live by. When I was in business school this quote made even more sense.

"Under promise, and over deliver."

Change has become a concept associated with danger, disruption, and intentional grief. Many books, lectures, and talks have been about change and change management. Hell, there are even people with degrees in change management. We have studied it from every angle, from business to psychology, and it impacts nearly every sector of industry all over the globe. It's been around for centuries, and yet, people still don't like change. You'd think we'd understand that by now, after centuries of evolution (which is essentially deliberate change through time). But no, we still hate the word no matter how much *change* has helped us.

I managed to introduce a little change in nearly every job I've ever had. Most was change that was necessary in order to keep operations going; others were supposed to be good change. I've even made my fair share of unwanted change. And every single time change was not easy.

As I stated previously, I studied change management and Lean Six Sigma in college. Both are unique subjects that include different concepts of change and how to implement them. Managing change is probably the one thing as a leader I've always dreaded. It's the one thing that is never easy, which is probably why I prefer to take the Lean approach to things.

Lean Management, however, is the process of creating value by optimizing resources. It's a long-term approach to continuous process improvement that often involves some change. However, Lean is more focused on searching for improvements and then making changes/alterations *only* if necessary to produce a better product. Something I always preached when we did Lean studies was that we weren't searching for change just to change something. We were searching for a purpose of change.

I have gone through many Lean studies just to decide not to change anything at all. And that's okay. Some things just don't need to be changed or improved at all. In the end, that's kind of the point. Lean became a practice because of Toyota, who was desperately trying to catch up in the auto industry. Toyota wasn't always the Toyota we see today, and they were searching for improvements. While doing this, in a nutshell, Toyota didn't change things just to change them. They studied processes and identified ways to change and improve, and only implemented them because it yielded results. Toyota eventually climbed the ladder and became not only a force to be reckoned with, but one of the top auto manufacturers in the world. All because they only implemented change when it made sense.

I believe all leaders should study some form of change management. Doesn't matter what it is, but they should study it. Not to better understand

CHAPTER 12

how to change things, but how change is done. To understand what it's like to go through change and give them the perspective of those who have to change. If you haven't gone over a change management process, then I suggest you do so immediately. Don't stop reading my book, but definitely find a change management process and study it.

The problem that leaders have with change is that they try to change things they see as needing change, and never stop to see if things actually need to be changed. Going back to the "If it ain't broke..." methodology, can you tell me why it's being changed?

The one thing that challenged me as a new leader in unfamiliar territory was changing things I didn't like. I didn't like them because I didn't understand them. Therefore, I wanted to change them to my preferences. That, in fact, is the wrong way of thinking.

Instead, I asked to be educated on the process. "Treat me like I'm dumb," I used to say. Explain to me like I was a brand-new person who did not know about the subject. From there I can ask questions and learn the process, even ask why certain things are done the way they are. I might have some excellent suggestions, or a better understanding of why things are done certain ways. Nothing was changed, and nothing broke.

Can you imagine changing something for the sake of changing it just to watch it break? That seems like a waste of time and poor decision making.

You want to break something really fast? Or piss off your teammates and employees? Change something for no reason at all. It will break and ruffle feathers immediately. You could move the coffeepot in the break room to another power outlet on the same damn countertop and it would mess with somebody. Why move it? Just because it looks nicer on the other outlet? That little ripple of change will send waves into the lives of others. And for what?

Change is a process, hence, why it's in the process part of the algorithm that requires agreement, faith, and trust. Change cannot come from just you. People will only see it as change because the boss said so. The best way to implement change is to involve people from the beginning.

> "The secret of change is to focus all of your energy, not on fighting the old, but on building the new."
>
> — *Socrates*

CHAPTER 13
THE 30-60-90 RULE

HERE'S THE TRUTH...

We think change is the first step in leadership. It's not. It's patience.

LEADERS DON'T STOP AND smell the roses. Instead, they pick the roses and get mad when there are no flowers left. Energetic leaders often forget how influential they are when first stepping into a new workplace. Being energetic and motivated is great, but do we really want to sacrifice quality for quantity? Nope, and that's why patience is the greatest leadership virtue.

First, let's understand this: you will never have enough time. Time is a commodity that we undervalue, yet desire heavily because we need more of it. It's the one thing we can't get more of. Time can be lost, but never really gained. You must respect time, as it's your best friend and worst enemy.

> "Great things come out of patience."
>
> — *Anonymous*

As a brand-new leader in a new workplace, what you say is law, even if you don't mean it. You could mention that red trash cans are weird and the next day they will replace all the trash cans with blue ones. Why? As a new leader, everybody is looking at you. If you speak, there's a chance they will take action, as impressing the new boss is a priority. They look at you as the boss, and everybody wants to know how the new boss thinks. Everybody wants to keep the boss happy. So, the littlest thing you say is actually like writing the law. It's seen and heard only for face value, not for deeper understanding. It's a big thing that many leaders don't understand. They speak but don't speak with context.

A big mistake leaders make is joining a new team and immediately making changes. Change is tough, as we've previously spoken about. You want to rule the workplace? Try taking a period of observation first. Remember, as the leader/boss/manager, you are the minority. There is only one of you. There are multiple, if not dozens of, team members. What you say and do influences all of them whether or not you mean it.

That's not to say that you should kick back and let things burn to the ground. Of course not. That would likely get you fired. There are going to be things you will have to address, problems that need your immediate attention.

Take care of those things ASAP.

Don't delay them. This rule isn't set in stone. It's designed to be a tool to help you integrate into your new role so that people see you as a leader. It's also to help your team get used to you, so don't rush things if you don't have to. Sometimes you have to get involved and fix something before it breaks, and that's fine. Other times you can let it go and observe. Use your judgment and handle business.

OBSERVATION

Observation is so important. Overseeing the entire landscape, battlefield, area of responsibility, environment, etc., tells you so much about the workplace without a spoken word. Observing performance, interaction, successes, failures, and personal habits all define the workplace. Take mental notes on all of this. It takes more than just one day; it takes consistent observation. As a leader, you should be just as much observer as you are speaker. I would argue you should probably talk less and observe more, as long as the team can communicate together. My personal leadership goal is to always get the team to where I facilitate and then observe. They work everything in between because I've guided, mentored, and supplied all the tools necessary for them to be successful, without my interruptions. They run it from there. I'm hands-on until It's time to be hands-off.

It will surprise you at how much the little things matter. The little things will make or break successful performance. I once watched my team arrive at work in the morning. I was the first one in the building, made my coffee, and sat and greeted every single one of them as they walked in for the day. You know what I noticed? Almost every single one of them walked in with breakfast, coffee, or a lunch box.

You know what that means? It means they are taking time every day to prepare a breakfast, coffee, and/or lunch for themselves. That preparation takes time, time that maybe my team doesn't have. They all have lives, kids, dogs, personal stuff going on. They have to squeeze in, making a quick bite to eat or preparing coffee to take to work. That's important to them, and time they don't necessarily have.

Same goes for daily operations. A watchful eye is not only to catch wrongdoings, but also to just learn the team. A confident leader knows all about their leadership and knows how to carefully implement it. That kind of implementation takes observation first. In other words, you observe that the peg is square, but the hole it fits into is round. It's simply not going to fit, right?

So you have two options:

1) Make it fit.

2) Mold it to fit.

You don't mold the peg to fit into the hole overnight. It takes time. So, why wouldn't you take the time to observe? My guess is because you don't have a philosophy to observe with. Today you are in luck, because I just happen to have one that I'm willing to share!

"A square peg doesn't fit into a round hole."

The above quote is something I said to my oldest son over and over again. He was a car guy, and still is. He understood mechanical stuff all the time, so this quote was fitting. During high school he often took the road that contained the most resistance, and I had to often watch him with a shaking head. I told him this quote and told him to think about it.

You spend so much time trying to make something work that won't, and then trying to shape the square peg into a circle so that it will fit. It's all a waste of time. Instead, you could just do it right the first time, and get the right shape. A round peg fits into a round hole almost every time. That strategy works better than being stubborn. Every time.

So, the next time you join a new team, try this concept/strategy on for size: 30-60-90. Once I learned it, this was the concept I used not just when I entered a new workplace, team, or organization, but also in my approach to new processes. Of course, if the new process allowed that kind of time, I took full advantage of it.

Let's break it down a bit further. Remember, the purpose of this process is to trust this process, trust each step, and OBSERVE. Observation is such an important part of this process and failure to do so will render the results you don't want. It won't be ideal—trust me. Patience and observation are key elements of this process, so trust it.

Chris Kyle was a US Navy SEAL sniper and one of the best in military history. His confirmed kill count rivals that of anybody who has ever gotten behind a rifle. Yes, he killed a lot of men. Men who wanted to kill even more. He killed well over one hundred people, but in the process saved thousands of lives. His job was to watch, observe, and take action as necessary to reduce threats.

As a leader, you need to be a sniper. Not in the typical way of taking people out, but in the manner of being patient and observing. Chris Kyle mentions in his book multiple times how he sat and watched for hours on end without pulling the trigger. His job was over watch, not necessarily engagement. Collecting intelligence and making observations was a large part of his job. He engaged as he needed to, but mostly, his job was to observe so he could protect. The information he collected by observation helped him, his team, and the leaders above him making better tactical decisions. Leaders need to do the same thing. Watch. Observe. Act. In that order.

A sniper is more than just a trigger-puller. These guys are tactical magicians. In FM 23-10, the official US Army Sniper field manual from 1994, the first chapter states:

> **1-1. Mission**
>
> The primary mission of a sniper in combat is to support combat operations by delivering long-range fire on selected targets... The secondary mission of the sniper is collecting and reporting battlefield information.

Now I was no sniper in my military career, but I deeply appreciate them. Their job is to literally sit and wait, knowing they very well might not have the opportunity to engage an enemy. That's probably a good thing, as it means nobody is in danger. However, they have another very critical job in collecting information. I learned this same kind of patience as a young kid hunting with my father and grandfather. And later on,

CHAPTER 13

as an adult hunting deer, I still came across this challenge. Finding the patience was never easy, but to those who wait, success will find them.

Entering a new job can be exciting, and excitement can lead to the desire to aggressively get to work. That can upset the balance, so be patient, and try out this 30-60-90 rule.

30 DAYS

Your first impression as a leader will last forever, not just for you, but for how you see things. It's about how people see you, and how you see them and all the things around them. The first thirty days should be used to get onboarded and in-processed with the organization. If it's a new process you are working with, observe and take notes. This can be very difficult to do because if the process isn't working, it will start to fail. Naturally, we want to keep things from failing, which saves our asses. But in this case, letting it fail is a good thing. How else are you going to get good feedback? Sometimes a process has to fail!

During the first thirty days, focus on learning names, job titles, duties, responsibilities, etc. Worry more about the people, the culture, and the environment than trying to understand the processes and rules. You should spend the first 30 days learning, so keep your suggestions to yourself. You want a suggestion? Keep a small notepad handy at all times. If you see or hear something you don't like, or question, write it down. A suggestion for something, or a great idea... write it down. There will be a time and a place for addressing these things soon. Just not inside thirty days. Obviously, if you see something that needs to be addressed right then, address it. No need to wait when employee safety or major consequences could have been avoided. Same thing with failure. If you see something about to critically fail and cause tons of harm to the organization and its people, step in and do something. But if it can fail and provide good feedback to future operations, as hard as it might be, let it fail.

> "Sometimes it's easier to learn what not to do,
> by doing what not to do."
>
> — Rick Pitino

60 DAYS

The first thirty days might be a struggle, but like I said previously, patience is key. The first thirty should see you getting ingrained in the organization or familiar with the process. If you haven't hung up the decorations on your office walls yet, don't worry—it's not that big of a deal. These next thirty days are all about interacting with the team and finding out more about them. Now is the time to ask serious questions and dig into what they do. It's, however, still not time for suggestions. Like a good detective, all you are doing is collecting evidence at this point. You are still one hundred percent learning and inquiring about things. Remember, you are also using this opportunity to get familiar with your team, so lean on them and their expertise to educate you. This will not only help educate you but will also build some trust between you and them.

The difference between these thirty days and the first thirty days is action. By now there will be some things that come up that require or ask for your action, direction, or guidance. I encourage you to make TEAM decisions and get the team players together to make these decisions. This is your chance to get everyone else to buy-in on who you are, so don't be afraid to huddle up and discuss. If you aren't taking heavy notes at this point, you should be. The next thirty days are going to be intense.

You've done a little bit of team building and inquiring and people are going to want to know more about you. Be patient. No need to go in guns blazing at all. If anything, now is the time to tell them a little about you on the personal side. Share your experiences, accomplishments, and hobbies. Tell them about your family, adventures, or anything else for that matter. In my experience, those that came right into an organization and just started shaking things up also spent the next several years trying to control the chaos and the dominoes that fell. Instead, you could spend ninety days investing in the organization and starting it off right or continuing its momentum of success.

> "Patience is a form of wisdom. It demonstrates that we understand and accept that the fact that sometimes things must unfold in their own time."
>
> — Jon Kabat-Zinn

90 DAYS

Two months into this experiment and I'm sure you are chomping at the bit to either change some things or kill the process. But now is not the time to lose your patience. If anything, it's more important now than ever. You've spent sixty days getting ingrained into the organization,

CHAPTER 13

finishing your paperwork, and collecting a few paychecks. Or watching the process, having discussions, and collecting great feedback. Now it's time to act.

Everyone wants to change things when they take over. You have to fight that urge and let at least sixty days pass first, doing your due diligence and observing first, while staying patient and trusting this process. Also, the team needs to get to know you. They can't try to juggle major changes while getting to know you and your leadership style. It just won't work. All they will learn to know you as is confusion and change, and it will be more chaos than change. Chaos with change is bad. You want effective change, so why are you orchestrating change using chaos? It just makes little sense. The two don't go together.

The below quote is something I heard my entire career. As a military force, we had our marching orders and knew what the mission needed. We all knew what we needed to do and often did it. And of course, things would change right in the middle of it. Either a politician or commanding general somewhere high up in the chain of command would change course or provide new guidance. It was often frustrating, but we had to stay the course and keep pushing. We had to be adaptable and ready for anything. That level of understanding in flexibility is what made us the best Air Force in the world. The quote has stuck with me even after my military days were over, because those six words mean so much more than just putting a plane into the sky. I don't remember where I first heard it, but it was a very common quote in my military career.

"Flexibility is the key to airpower."

Don't undervalue observing your team. Patience is a virtue. Dedicate time to it. It will amaze you at what you see, and what you will find out. But if you try to observe on your own terms, you will observe very little. Be flexible and try new tactics. You can learn a lot, see a lot, and really understand the team dynamics, no matter how large or small. It's very important to take the time to observe. As we continue to build our leadership algorithm, make sure your requirements include observation, but in a way that means something to the team. You don't want this part of your algorithm to be a challenge for the team.

CHAPTER 14
STRATEGY

HERE'S THE TRUTH...

Strategies must have a purpose.

HAVING A STRATEGY is easier said than done, and taking the time to make a strategy is worth its weight in gold. You must invest time in order to achieve results.

I've met plenty of people who prefer to do things by the seat of their pants, or on the fly. They simply prefer to decide in the moment. That's their strategy. Nothing wrong with it, as it's their strategy. I prefer a more thought-out and detailed plan. But that's just me. I've worked with several leaders who could construct and define a long-term strategy, and I've also worked with leaders who had a very general strategy and an incredible ability to make significant decisions on the fly. Your strategy is simply what works for you, and what works for people around you.

Remember that.

> "Strategy is a fancy word for coming up with a long-term plan and putting it into action."
>
> — *Ellie Pidot*

I have no clue who Ellie Pidot is, but when I saw the quote above, I knew it was gold. It makes so much sense and hits the nail right on the head. Turns out when she said this she was the vice-president of strategy at Medtronic. Medtronic is a medical technology, services, and solutions company founded in 1949 in Minnesota. Their headquarters are now in Dublin, Ireland. I've done a great deal of business with Medtronic back on active duty working as a logistician in medical supply. It's great to see a company with an executive focused so heavily on strategy. That's probably why they were named the largest medical device company in the world back in 2018. With headquarters in Ireland and Minnesota, plus several subsidiary companies, it's no wonder. As of 2020, Medtronic was a Fortune 500 company.

Strategy is important. No other way to say it. There were times in my military career where we had little strategy and just had to wing it, but it wasn't optimal. Other times we had plenty of time to develop a strategy and over-thought it. It happens. Regardless, we had to make decisions, and often make them quickly. I firmly believe members of the military are some of the best decision makers when it comes to quick decisions.

Outstanding leaders know a strategy is necessary, but they also understand that a large blanket strategy won't always work, especially if that strategy is too specific. Yes, big blanket strategies can work. Yes, they will work if you allow for flexibility. Yes, if you have a prominent leader who has a flexible strategy and is open to new things and innovation, you can really bend, twist, and manipulate a strategy to fit. The problem is, leaders either have a bold strategy that their ego won't allow to be flexible, or they have too broad of a strategy and it also won't allow for any kind of flexibility. And if they are flexible, you could end up spending more time adjusting and making changes than you would on the initial strategy. It's tough, and in both situations, leaders are afraid of making mistakes or being wrong. I got a truth for you. As a leader you will be wrong... a lot. It's part of the job! You can't lead effectively being afraid of failure or making mistakes. Those things are inevitable.

For years, I struggled with my own leadership philosophy. I knew I had one but didn't know how to communicate it. How do you tell people what you are thinking in a way that they will understand? Often times, the stuff in my head sounds great to me, but not always to everyone else. The madness upstairs isn't always ready for primetime TV. It takes time to formulate your strategy, and even more time to accurately articulate it to others in a manner in which they will understand. The last thing you want to do is introduce a plan that falls flat on its face.

CHAPTER 14

That's when I came up with the leadership algorithm that combines effort and process to equal progress. It wasn't a fluke. I struggled with this for a long time. In fact, this book went through at least fifty different drafts before I nailed down what I really wanted to talk about. It took multiple years before my vision became somewhat clear. It took even longer before I finally figured out my concept of a leadership algorithm.

When I first started writing, I didn't have a strategy—I just wrote. I thought that would work. Nope. It was crap on paper. I then sought help and attended an online writing conference. It was more for fiction than nonfiction, but it taught me strategy and how to get organized. Plus, it taught me how to write fiction, which is something I'm passionate about. So it killed two birds with one stone and put me on a course toward building my own strategy for writing. What I didn't know was that it also put me on a path toward creating my own leadership strategy and helping me define it.

I also reached out and got a brand coach. Communicating what you are thinking into words, pictures, and impactful influences isn't as easy as it sounds. With the help of my brand coach, I found my inner voice and learned how to communicate it. Over the course of several months, my brand coach changed my life. I was so confident in what I was saying that I literally hit delete on a draft of this very book and rewrote it over a weekend. Almost thirty-thousand words in two days, a complete overhaul of the concept. However, it birthed what you are reading today. That new version was the version I submitted to my publisher, who then bought off on it and presented me with a contract. Asking for help is a good thing!

Let's debunk strategy for a minute. Many people think a strategy is a detailed plan that outlines every step of the way, and charts for contingencies. Errors throw the strategy off and ruin the plan. That would be wrong because a plan is called a plan for a reason. Strategies are concepts that drive you toward creating a detailed plan, helping you stick to your purpose while developing and carrying out the plan. Strategies are meant to be long-term things, a guiding principle for the journey. Strategy keeps you from winging it or flying by the seat of your pants. Both concepts only work part of the time, and normally only in short-term situations. In my experience, winging it worked less than half the time and wasn't an excellent strategy at all. It works for some, but it is not a long-term solution. In tight situations, taking a few seconds to make an educated decision has been, in my experience, better than winging it.

I faced quick decisions and tight deadlines on more than one occasion in my military career, and an educated guess was often better than anything else. By educated guess, I'm talking about a quick consultation with the experts or your team and quickly making a decision or plotting a way forward. Facts or guidance backed the decision up, but not with enough time to analyze the pros and cons. It's the best-case scenario, in a scenario that doesn't allow for much time. Of course, it's not optimal, but it's better than nothing. And nothing is better than taking the time to build a long-term strategy, which is, and will more than likely be, the most optimal option.

I'll give you an example. In one of my previous endeavors, we had a terrible outlook on the budget, income, and how revenue worked. Not everyone involved had a business background, and we all didn't communicate well. We collectively needed to find ways to drive in more revenue. The problem wasn't the ability to have revenue, as we had all the pieces in place to get revenue but just weren't using them correctly to drive more revenue or return revenue through returning customers. There was a "it should come to us" mentality, and we weren't actively trying to gain new or repeat customers.

The financial situation was a nightmare, and nobody had any kind of discipline or strategy when it came to money. On a daily basis, we spent more money than we earned, and it was driving us further and further into debt. As a leadership team, myself, my boss, and our bigger boss put our heads together and decided we needed a plan. I used a template given to me by our boss and heavily modified it (and I mean heavily). What I did was build a concept of operations (CONOPS) for the entire organization.

What we lacked was returning revenue. Money was coming in the door, but only with new customers. Returning customers weren't all that common, and we had a horrible plan for turning new customers into repeat customers. It was obvious, as we didn't put out an excellent product, and then blamed it on poor support from the customers and business partners. There was no accountability in our efforts and that had to change. Being satisfied with mediocre was no longer acceptable.

So, I drafted up a new strategy that would focus on quality, feedback, and recommended changes. If we wanted to capture customers and have them come back, we had to capture their feedback and experiences. We could no longer assume they were satisfied; we had to prove satisfaction.

I divided the new CONOPS into four areas. The first two were marketing and planning. I found that we did two things terribly—spreading the word and then putting together a quality plan. We often

CHAPTER 14

started advertising for the event or program a few weeks before the start date. It didn't allow enough time for our customer market to mark the calendar and make plans. It was always too last minute, and our participation rates showed it. A review of our marketing program by an outside source discovered and proved a lot of the things we knew already and provided us with some great tools for the road ahead.

The goal was to find new ways to market our businesses and create a strategic planning working group so we could get back to the business of working together and planning at a higher level. We wanted to grab the attention of our customers around forty-five- to sixty-days out and give them a reason to mark their calendars. The buzz around the event would be on their mind for well over a month and would give us the first chance to occupy space on their calendar.

Our quality of plans was poor, and often not even documented. It was a lot of winging it, and it just would not cut it anymore. The accountability was on us, and we had to produce. The problem was nobody communicated, and the plans were often just informal conversations and emails. There was no organization, discipline, or accountability. Not to mention, these informal plans didn't start until we finished the previous event, allowing for at the max two or three weeks of actual planning to work on the event. The team couldn't juggle multiple events in the planning stages at one time, and we needed a better strategy. We were literally putting things together at the last minute, and it showed.

The new rule was no event or operation would be conducted unless a quality marketing plan and operations/event plan was in place, documented, and approved by the boss. This meant that events we normally planned in about thirty days now got extended out to six months. The focus was on quality, not quickness. Taking our time was going to iron out the kinks and present a quality event or operation, which meant (hopefully) higher customer satisfaction, and therefore, the potential for more returning customers. Just like a website, we want to answer those three big questions: What do you do? How can you make their life better? How can they buy from you?

Parts three and four focused on after actions. What we wanted to know and understand was how the customer felt about the experience. How was their food? Was the service good? What would they change? What would they like to see? We spent months gathering information, despite pushback from some of the managers. We turned this information into changes, both good and bad. It was a tough road, but the changes turned new customers into repeat customers, and more faith in our products and services. In a simple, yet effective, four-part plan, we had a concept of operations for the entire organization. It worked even for places within our business that weren't involved with sales. Change isn't easy, and neither was this. It took almost a year, but we saw improvement and eventually started making more instead of throwing it away.

As a leader, you have to have the long-term vision, as not everyone else will. You also have to have faith in that vision, as there will be doubters and people who lose faith.

> "Doubt kills more dreams than failure ever will."
> — *Karim Seddiki*

CHAPTER 15
COMMUNICATION, PART 1

HERE'S THE TRUTH...

You don't communicate for you; you communicate for everybody else.

LEADERS SPEAK. It's plain and simple. If they don't speak, they aren't really leaders. I've never met a quiet leader. There have been leaders who spoke few words, but the words they spoke had influence and impact. But in my experience, leaders who don't communicate openly and often have a very hard time succeeding. You have to speak up.

But just because you can speak and communicate doesn't mean you are good at it. You might think you are, but you aren't the one who gets to determine that. The people you lead will be a direct reflection on how you communicate as a leader. There have been entire books, college degrees, and ongoing discussions about communication, yet nobody has fully mastered it. Communication is a developing thing that needs constant attention.

In this first part of Communication, I want to talk about the principles of delivery and tone. Before you get into delivering a message, you must understand how to deliver it. Without proper delivery, even great news can fall flat. Conveying a message takes skill, and how it's conveyed can dictate the effectiveness.

During my time in the military, I saw many leaders fail to understand how to deliver when they communicated. Some of them acted excited when they shouldn't have, giving off a sense of fake excitement. Some also didn't seem as excited when delivering good news, and some acted to upset when delivering bad news. When the tone and delivery didn't match the message being delivered, it caused more problems than it offered answers. The smallest bit of news can have a significant impact on operations, both good and bad. But there is a way to deliver that news for maximum influence and appropriate impact. Nothing worse than delivering news and people reacting like they could not care less. Understanding your tone when delivering through communication is important.

"Communicate. Even when it's uncomfortable or uneasy."

— Anonymous

I like to call communication the silent killer, because without communication you can kill a team or an organization overnight. If communication is silent, it's a deadly killer. It's also something that people spend decades trying to master, and never fully do. Communication is such a tough concept to master, and it is also arguably one of the most important things in leadership.

Leaders are often misunderstood because when they speak, they don't speak with context. Lack of context makes the message dead on arrival, and of course the delivery was at fault. The meat and potatoes are there, but nothing else is. There is a lack of context, and therefore no facts or guidance included in the message. It's something leaders find themselves failing at, myself included during my career.

Nobody can read your mind, so what you say has to be more complex than what you are thinking. In your head, a message is simple and to the point because you understand it and understand it well. But the people who you are delivering it to don't always understand it. You have to explain and provide details. The more details the better, and you can always read the room and scale back. If you can see that people are understanding, you can start getting right to the point. Time is your friend; you can use as much of it as you need to make your point.

I struggle with providing context because I would think of it in my head, conceptualize it, and be ready to explain it. But when I did, I would keep it short and sweet because I already understood it, so I didn't feel the need to repeat it. However, I failed to realize that there are two parts to the communication audience: 1) yourself and 2) everybody else. I had already explained it to myself, so the internal need

CHAPTER 15

to comprehend it had already happened. As a person who strives for efficiency, duplication is not in my nature. So I don't repeat myself often and when I do, I get frustrated. It was, and sometimes still is, something I have to work on. But more importantly, I need to be aware of it and provide deeper context. Nobody is going to read my mind.

Knowing who your audience is can sometimes be a challenge. But we bring it up because it's very important in leadership. Why? Because your communication should center on who you are talking to. For example, when I was in the Air Force, I spoke to my subordinate military members a certain way. It was more direct, more authoritative, and with higher expectations. As for the civilians I worked with? Not so much. I was still direct and authoritative, but my tone was different and often my delivery was more strategic. I could tell my military folks to go unload a truck and they would just go and do it. That's kind of the way in the military. But my civilians? As much as I loved them, I had to ask nicely. The direct style of leadership would not work with them. I had to catch those flies with honey instead of vinegar. Know your audience. Read the room. Deliver appropriately for maximum impact.

The first part of that audience is yourself, as you speak to yourself all the time. Thoughts develop in your head and become actionable, and your brain keeps them inside for your own needs. Not everything you think of is communicated to someone else, as it's a discussion between you and your conscience. Perhaps your conscience is actually the middleman between the little devil on one shoulder and the little angel on the other. I remember when I was little that appeared in cartoons all the time. It shows the clear dynamic that we deal with when making decisions ourselves, and how our conscious works with us on organizing and filtering the information we develop. Bottom line: what you think sounds good often only sounds good to you. It will sound different to people you speak it to.

The second part of that audience is what I want to focus on when it comes to your leadership algorithm. We are to the point now that we are working on that process part, combining the efforts into the processes, and preparing for results. However, ineffective communication can stifle that in a heartbeat. Remember, you don't communicate for you—you communicate for everybody else. That gets lost on people all too often. Communication is not to hear yourself, but for others to hear you.

> "Coming together is a beginning. Keeping together is progress. Working together is success."
>
> — *Henry Ford*

This audience is different because you don't know them like you know yourself. Not only that, but you hear yourself in a different tone. So, when communicating with this side of the audience, you have to be much more aware of how you speak, as your delivery, tone, style, and words all represent the information. This part of communication is an absolute art form. In fact, it took me years to realize my tone and delivery weren't optimal. Messages will fall on deaf ears if someone does not communicate properly. People can see through fake expressions, and they will render even the best news irrelevant. Communication to others must be authentic.

When in charge, you must act like you are in charge. You need to believe it as well. However, that is all for internal things. That's the stuff you tell yourself in those certain moments of bravery or courage. You don't say those things in your communication. One of the worst things I ever heard a leader say repeatedly is, "I'm in charge." Well, if you have to say it often, you aren't as in charge as you think.

Delivery, approach, and tone are important. You can literally say the exact same sentence in two different ways and get two different results. If I tell my staff to turn in their timecards by the end of the day in a harsh and direct tone, many of them will probably ignore me. It appears as if the boss is just shouting orders. I expect they will get it done and do it because I said so. I've provided no value and failed to acknowledge the importance of the task. The box just needs to be checked so we can say we've accomplished it.

I can't just walk in and shout that out. It won't have much effect, if any at all. And more than likely it will condition them all to ignore me when I raise my voice or use a negative tone. My approach will turn them off to listening to me. Long-term, that's not good at all.

Now, if I walk into the work section and politely ask for everyone's attention, excusing myself for interrupting, and professionally ask everyone to please turn in their timecards by the end of the day, more people are going to listen. I'd then exit and thank them, while apologizing again for interrupting. Probably even throw in a, "I appreciate you guys. Have a great Friday." For one, I interrupted them all apologetically, acknowledging that I understand they are busy, and I value their time. Second, I solidified that I am the boss, delivering an important message that should be listened to and acted upon after receipt. I did that without raising my voice or banging my fist. I then exited while thanking them for doing what they are supposed to do, and apologized again for interrupting (even though it was necessary). Some might find this method weak, or even lacking authority. Authority doesn't have to come from your voice; it comes from the message that you deliver. This manner is strategic as it encourages action. Even in the military, this can be an effective means of communication. Not all of us yell and scream orders while wearing a uniform. Some of the most respected leaders speak effectively, with a strategy that demands action and respect. It's simple, and if you cast your ego to the side, it works.

Once I learned how tone and delivery worked, I thought about situations just like the example above, often consulting with my leadership and mentors first. I found an outstanding balance of maintaining my discipline and status as the boss while meshing with my team and the people I led. My change in tone, delivery, and approach to things yielded way more results than the dictator-like approach to being in charge. I didn't have to shout orders or snap my fingers. People listened because they respected what I had to say, and they respected me.

> "The loudest voice in a room is seldom the wisest."
>
> — Matshana Dhlwayo

Mastering communication is a constant labor. Just when you think you understand it and have a good strategy down, it changes. I worked on it for years, and I'm still working on it. And that's just verbal communication. We haven't even discussed written communication, which has a lot of the same principles and twice the challenges.

Written communication is tricky. Much more emotion and interpretation are involved in written communications. Written communication should be used for quick and precise communication. If you have to get into a lengthy explanation, you are best off calling a meeting and explaining it to everyone face-to-face. This was a lesson I learned a long time ago. Long drawn-out emails don't get read. They also don't get interpreted in the manner in which you typed it. It's ineffective communication for something you have to explain in more than a few sentences. It's a tool for communication, not the primary method. Remember that.

If I have to scroll down and take nearly ten minutes out of my day to read your email, I most likely won't get through it all. And if I do, I'll likely have to re-read it and highlight the important points or calls to action. If that's the case, and you can't say it in a few sentences, do it face-to-face. It's just better and more effective. Type up some talking points, print them off, and call a face-to-face meeting. The delivery will be better and more authentic. Your body language and attitude can help convey the message, and you can get instant feedback on how the message was perceived. Lazy leaders rely on email. And as leaders, when we communicate, we want to be authentic and effective.

Another lesson learned: never rely on technology to do people things. I once used email to send messages I wasn't brave enough to say in person. If someone was late, instead of talking to them privately, I'd send them an email about it. I considered my job done at that point. It didn't matter if they read the email or not. I sent the message, so the matter was considered resolved. On many occasions that mindset has come back to haunt me. That type of communication isn't very personal, and it's often not as effective. I can tell you from experience.

Don't rely on technology to do that stuff. It's lazy, and it's not leadership. Instead, use it as a tool. Use email for short messages that can be instantly effective and understood. Use it to follow up on a meeting so people can reference it later. You can even use it as a reminder, but never, ever, use it as your primary method of communication.

Leadership is addressing the issue head-on, professionally, so that the people involved can see the emotion and body language. Those things help deliver the message and express the importance. All things an email can't do.

Communication isn't easy. At times, it will be uncomfortable. Other times, it will fail. Leaders must keep trying. Lazy communication will equal lazy leadership, and lazy leadership will equal lazy habits and a culture of undetailed amateurs. Influential leaders know how to communicate, both verbally and personally. Communication should be at the top of your priority list, right next to the million other things you have to do. Leadership isn't easy or for the faint of heart. But learning to be a great communicator will ease the headaches—I promise!

> "Communication is crucial to a leader's success. He/she can accomplish nothing unless they can communicate effectively."
>
> — *Tony Robbins*

CHAPTER 16
COMMUNICATION, PART 2

HERE'S THE TRUTH...

If you think you've said enough, you probably haven't.

ONE OF THE MOST COMMON issues I see with leaders, and have seen over the course of my career, is failing to properly communicate what they want to say. Way too often a leader communicates only half of what they are actually thinking, leaving many things unsaid. The problem is that the expectations are still the same despite not delivering the full message. They become frustrated because they left things on the table, and actions after the delivery fell short of expectations. All because of unsatisfactory communication.

The other side of communication is self-fulfillment. Many politicians practice this, preferring to hear themselves speak over speaking to others. If you are impressed with how you sound when you speak, you need to try again. Communication is not for you; it's for others.

In your head, with your own ears, you will always sound good. Your brain automatically goes into defense mode and tries to convince you otherwise. Just because it sounds good doesn't mean it is good. It could be horrible. The way people hear your speech differs from how you formulate it. It's just a natural habit. However, some people are okay with that and like to hear what they have to say. This is typical egocentric leadership, speaking to hear oneself as opposed to influence others through speech. The best thing to do is put yourself in the shoes of your audience and ask how you would want the information delivered. Content and context are important.

> "Communication works for those who work at it."
>
> — John Powell

In the second part of communication, I want to talk about context. Fellow author Jon Hinderliter wrote a book called, *The Death of Content as King*, a fantastic book about marketing and how media content once thrived and now data analytics rules all. (It's award-winning only six months after its release—you must pick it up!) So taking a page from his book, I want to state that in communication, *Context is King*.

For leaders, managers, or just people running an operation, delivering your full context is the critical starting point. Your first thoughts deliver guidance, direction, and even rules of engagement (ROEs). If you fail to fully deliver your entire message in a manner in which people can understand and go forward with, you've doomed the operation from the very start. And you have nobody else to blame but you. You left things on the table.

I look back at Thomas Levitt's *Marketing Myopia* when I think about communication, as communicating the right thing is the point Levitt was trying to make. For instance, he takes the petroleum industry and uses it for a good example. For the most part when we mention petroleum, we think of gas and oil. We need gas and oil for our cars to run, and to run properly. Without gas, the cars won't run; without oil, the engine will seize up. Failure to put both into our cars yields no results, or in the case of my sixteen-year-old son, it means a seized-up engine dead on the side of the road, down the street from the local police department's training compound. The point is, we commonly associate petroleum as gas or oil.

Marketing tells us not just what it is, but what else it is and how that affects our lives. It delivers a full range of information, influencing us to make a purchase or support a cause. The importance in marketing is connecting to the audience so that the message will influence them to take action. Marketing is a form of communication and has mastered the ability to deliver.

What we should know petroleum as is *energy*.

CHAPTER 16

Why? Because petroleum is energy. It's energy for our cars, trains, machinery, manufacturing, and a long, long list of many other things. Petroleum is much more than just gas and oil. It's energy that supports so many things and has so many forms. Without petroleum we wouldn't have ninety percent of the goods we have today. The industry is enormous, not just because we have over 276 million cars on the road today, according to the Bureau of Transportation Statistics (2019), but because petroleum products have been used in everything from making groceries to powering the latest rocket-carrying satellites we blast into orbit. Petroleum is more than gas or oil for our cars. It really does power our lives.

What does that have to do with communication? Well, it's simple: the petroleum industry failed to accurately communicate what they were, and therefore got labeled as just gas and oil. They left part of their message on the table. All we as consumers relate to them is automobiles.

Now the petroleum industry has a bad rap, and people view them as just money-hungry executives getting rich off of three- to six-dollar-a-gallon gas. Hard to argue when gas is over three dollars a gallon, but in reality there's much more to it than that. Now the industry is fighting an uphill battle to be viewed as pioneers in the energy industry, innovators of how petroleum might change our lives in the future. Gas prices can fluctuate like a flick of a light switch, a temperament so fragile that the slightest political move can send it into motion.

When someone mentions ExxonMobil, I bet most think gas or oil, or maybe both. But did you know ExxonMobil has carbon capture technology to help reduce emissions? Or that they have a program that is designing a renewable diesel fuel? These programs are not only in response to the demand for lower emissions and better fuel mileage, but also for the fact that it might be a very long time until we actually see fully electric semi-trucks that can haul large loads long distances. In return, we need more efficient fuels that can reduce emissions. If you go to ExxonMobil's website, all of these keywords are apparent. Seldom do they mention gas.

So when speaking about your leadership, your philosophy, and your strategy, remember context is king. Plan what you want to say, and then say it. Don't leave things on the table. Never assume the entire message will be understood if you didn't deliver it all. What you say, even in small doses, can say a lot. It can have tremendous effects on people, so choose your words wisely. When you communicate, you want to say exactly what needs to be said, not always what you want to say. Don't be too narrow-minded and pin yourself in a small box. Leadership isn't small, so don't think small.

> "Leadership doesn't exist in a vacuum. It manifests in a context. These contexts are as dynamic as the personalities, stakes, culture, and information available."
>
> — Author Michael M. Rose

Context and delivery were probably the biggest leadership lessons I ever learned. First, learning to deliver a message in a respectful tone, without sounding like a jerk, was eye-opening. Finding out how you actually sound, versus how you think you sound, is life-changing. Next, it's about context.

When you are in charge or in a position of authority or leadership, you often have to wear a lot of hats. Most of my career has been like that, with me trying to juggle primary duties and a few dozen other secondary duties. When you are that loaded down, you do things like cut corners and find ways to keep things short and sweet. However, that's where the problems are found.

In busy situations, we cut things short in order to save time, sacrificing quality on behalf of saving a little time. We label it as efficiency, but it's really a recipe for disaster. In the kitchen, especially one like Gordon Ramsey works in, time is probably the most important thing outside of communication. Time determines if a dish is cooked properly, undercooked, or overcooked. And have you seen him lose his mind when something is overcooked? It's not nearly as bad as when something is undercooked. Simply stated, you don't bring him a raw dish. He'd much rather you do it right the first time than waste time doing it again because you messed up the first try.

Now you are wasting more time to redo the work than you would have if you just did it properly the first time. Timing is everything, so if you are short on time, get more organized in order to be efficient. Don't cut things out, because that's when you stop communicating, and you should never sacrifice communication. Instead, take a minute to get organized before pressing forward. Sloppy organization will cause sloppy communication.

Speaking of sloppy communication, let's get back to context. When you are unorganized and short on time, you cut corners. When you cut corners, what happens? You get in a hurry and leave out critical details. These left-out details can lead to mediocre or less-than-expected results,

CHAPTER 16

and whose fault is that? As a leader, the finger has to be pointed back at you. There are no shortcuts in leadership or communication, so why put either of those on the chopping block? Don't leave things on the table. Plan, execute, and deliver.

> "There are no shortcuts to success."
>
> — Annika Sorenstam

A valuable lesson I learned in my leadership journey was communicating and communicating precisely. That means, think about what you want to say, and then say it. Don't leave things out for the sake of time, or because you believe people will just understand. When speaking as a leader, break things down to their basic level so that the entire crowd understands. A great military leader of mine once said, "You have to speak to the dumbest person in the room." It sounds rude and insulting, but in all honesty, it's the truth. You can't speak to the average. The average means that some people will understand, and others won't. Some people will get it perfectly and other people will get lost. It's a 50/50 scenario. However, if you speak to the "dumbest" person in the room, that means you're breaking it down to its simplest form, presenting the message for all to hear. If you can't speak to everyone, how effective can you really be?

Marketing is very much the same way. I've studied marketing concepts while working on both my graduate and doctoral degrees. A common theme I've found is context, and how you reach your audience. In order to relay the full context of your message, you must break it down to the simplest, most direct form possible and target a specific audience. With the wrong format targeting a specific audience, you could still miss, so knowing your audience and then tailoring your context to them is key for maximum understanding.

When I was the director of operations for a small Air Force squadron composed of a restaurant, a bowling center, two childcare centers, a twenty-eight-room lodging facility, and various other departments, I didn't speak to each department in the same manner. The context I needed to deliver to each of them was often different, and it needed to be. I had to know my audience.

Half the squadron was business-centric; the other half was customer-care-centric. We didn't run the restaurant the same way we ran the childcare centers. We just didn't, and we couldn't. And in return, the context they needed to deliver to me was in their terms, so I had to learn childcare, human resources, and hotel management language. I couldn't expect them to learn my language without learning theirs, so I absorbed as much context of theirs as I could and pressed forward.

Communication is only as successful as the least successful communicator in the room. Don't cut corners on communication and let your context suffer. It will only create more stressors than solutions. If your team, or the people you lead, have to ask questions after you speak, you aren't communicating right. You should leave them with understanding, clarity, and confidence.

"Good communication is the bridge between confusion and clarity."

— *Nat Turner*

In this first part of Communication, I want to talk about the principles of delivery and tone. Before you get into delivering a message, you must understand how to deliver it. Without proper delivery, even great news can fall flat. Conveying a message takes skill, and how it's conveyed can dictate the effectiveness.

PART 3
PROGRESS

Effort + Process = <u>PROGRESS</u>

The last part of the algorithm is PROGRESS, or, in other words, the RESULTS. Process as defined by Webster's dictionary is:

progress (noun)
1. A forward or onward movement
2. To move forward
3. To develop to a higher, better, or more advanced stage

Progress is a word that has multiple definitions. We can use it in multiple manners, with multiple intended results. The above definition is just a few of what Webster's dictionary provided, and I picked those because it accurately describes the use of progress in the context of the algorithm, and the last section of this book.

The last part of the algorithm is *progress,* because after putting the effort (input) into the processes (process), we should start seeing some progress (results). The problem many leaders run into at this point is understanding the results. Most expect perfection or excellent results, but that's just not how this works. More often than not, you will put in monumental work and effort and get mediocre results. It happens all the time. What you do with those results determines the levels of long-term success. Crawl before you walk. Nothing worth having comes quickly. Success is a grind.

Patience is the critical key in leadership. Did you achieve some progress/results? Good! Although we aren't expecting perfection, we are expecting progress. Total failure would be not achieving a result at all, meaning the steps taken need an overhaul. Remember when I said, "Perfection is a fool's definition of success," all the way back at the beginning of the book? Well, let it marinate a little more right now.

What we want to do with progress is to understand it and build upon it. So many leaders analyze the results so that they can try to find the unique advantage that made it work, happy with the results no matter the quality. Over time, all that mentality gets you is mediocre and average success. It's just like an entrepreneur trying to make their mark in the world. There are no set hours, no set expectations. You will get the amount of success out of being an entrepreneur that you put into being an entrepreneur. That likely means late nights, long days, and frustrating times. But time will endure, and so should you. Time will also reward people who keep working, keep trying, and try to be better every time.

Instead, let's analyze the progress and find out why things worked, and how we can improve on them. In this section, we are going to focus on active listening, accountability, culture, and all things with leadership growth. The point of progress is not to measure how successful it was, but to understand why it was successful and what we can do to make it more successful. Leadership is an always-developing thing, and your personal leadership will be no different.

Patience is key here, as it might feel like you are taking two steps backwards. In reality, you aren't, as you are really just taking a good, hard look at the effort and processes it took to get here—willing to analyze it and make it better. Influential leaders don't become influential leaders through experience alone; they become influential leaders through a combination of experience and lessons learned. Leaders Learn Daily (LLD). It might be slow; it might be frustrating. But don't quit. Now is the time to really grow and standardize results.

"Progress may be slow, but quitting won't make it any faster."

— *Anonymous*

CHAPTER 17
AAR – ACTIVE LISTENING, ACCOUNTABILITY, AND RESPONSIBILITY

HERE'S THE TRUTH...

Accountability and responsibility are a "we" thing.

LIKE A LOT OF ACRONYMS, AAR has several definitions. In the military it means After Action Review/Reports. These reviews and reports, which we will discuss shortly, are critical pieces to military processes. They provide retrospective analysis on a sequence of events, goals, or previously undertaken events or processes. In the corporate world, the term and process have become a standard practice. In simple terms, they are tools used to get feedback and information after an operation, mission, or an exercise (simulation). The lessons learned from the successes, failures, and issues that arise are invaluable parts of continuous growth.

On one hand, AAR means after actions, but it also can mean Active listening, Accountability, and Responsibility. In this chapter, we are going to discuss the leadership meaning of it, and how active listening, accountability, and responsibility play critical roles in progress. Having a thorough knowledge of how AAR—both definitions—can help you as a leader will continue to grow your leadership and develop your algorithm.

Naturally, as humans we listen intending to provide a response. That's just how we are naturally wired. As we listen, we are already formulating thoughts and potential responses. And that is the entire problem with listening—we are already thinking about a response while someone is talking. It's just a naturally occurring process. However, when we listen to respond, we aren't listening to acquire new information or perspectives.

How is this remedied? Well, it takes some practice. Active listening is a concept that every leader should practice, and one that is important to your leadership development and to tailoring your leadership style.

ACTIVE LISTENING

Active listening is the concept of listening completely before formulating a response. The Center for Creative Leadership describes active listening as "a valuable technique that requires the listener to thoroughly absorb, understand, respond, and retain what's being said." They define six big active listening skills as 1) paying attention, 2) withholding judgment, 3) reflecting, 4) clarifying, 5) summarizing, and 6) sharing.

Naturally, as humans we listen with our mouths and prepare to talk. As someone is talking to us, we are naturally thinking about how to respond or what to say next. It distracts us from what is being said and from absorbing it all in. In a basic conversation, you are listening and breaking down what is being said and analyzing it for what it is and how you can use it. In a discussion, you are breaking spoken words down and planning your response.

If you are busy planning what you want to respond with, how are you taking in everything that is being said? There's no time to reflect or to withhold judgment. In fact, you aren't reflecting on it at all, as you haven't even heard the entire message yet! You also don't withhold judgment and are, in fact, judging the entire time. Without active listening, you have no opportunity at all to just hear the message.

The challenge as a leader, who is often responsible for many things, is trying to trust and actively listen. It's incredibly hard because we are defensive people by nature. We protect ourselves from hearing information we don't want to hear, or that might be dangerous/hazardous to us. As leaders, again, responsible for people, processes, and even money, we are on the defensive in order to protect what we handle. Actively listening to every message being spoken to you, not passing judgment, and giving yourself time to reflect on it is a difficult task. However, once you master it, you can truly hear and see all the facts, truths, and the good, the bad, and the ugly of your operations without bias. Just the facts; just the truth (like it or not). Active listening will help you become a more efficient leader and accurate decision maker. Use it as a tool and hear what is being said, not what you want to hear.

AFTER ACTION REVIEW/REPORTS

Now that you understand what active listening is, you can conduct an AAR to discuss after actions. It's critical that during this process you at least have a grasp on what active listening is so that you can appropriately hear the information being shared. This meeting is a chance to get specific feedback from the people involved and should be used as an opportunity to let people speak honestly, and for you as a leader to hear that honesty.

In the military we used a term called AAR, which stood for "After Action Review/Report." It was a process in which, directly after an event, exercise (simulation), or project, everyone involved sat down and discussed how it went. Included in this review/report were essentially the good, the bad, and the ugly. The chance to discuss and break down how things went is immensely important for growth and for correcting issues, especially when multiple people, departments, or agencies are involved. AAR is a critical piece to military operations, as it could mean the difference between life and death. These meetings are for honesty and truth, no sugarcoating BS here. What worked today can help us be better tomorrow, and what didn't work today can be corrected for tomorrow, saving lives, and keeping people safe.

As a leader, conducting an AAR right after an event is important. It doesn't matter if you are active duty, former active duty now serving in the civilian world, or a civilian with no military experience at all. For leaders at all levels, AAR should be in your memory forever. Tattoo it on your forehead if you have to. Just never forget about it. Feedback is the most important thing in the world for growth. Growth for both you as a leader and your team requires feedback. Truthful feedback.

ACCOUNTABILITY

Accountability is possibly the most important thing of leadership. In actuality, this could probably be its own chapter, maybe even its own book. For the sake of time, we are only going to discuss how accountability affects you as a leader in leadership situations.

Accountability works two ways. One, it works as a tool for you as a leader to keep people doing their job and doing it well, as well as being aware and responsible for their actions. This works in multiple ways because their work, work ethic, and behaviors/attitude all impact the work center and team. Holding them accountable for these actions and behaviors can make or break a team. How you hold them accountable is up to you, but I highly suggest being less of a ruler and more of a mentor/coach.

When I coached middle-school-level football in a competitive league, our goal was to win the championship every year. I loved working with the kids, especially because they had competitive spirits, and it was a competitive game. We coached, mentored, and tried to grow these kids as much as possible. I was their coach and mentor, and to them, almost like a friend. We were tough at times, and a little less tough in other times. But I had to hold each and every player accountable for their actions and performance. Sometimes that meant sending them to run some sprints, run laps, or hit the stadium for some stairs. Other times it meant dropping them down for some push-ups when they talked while I was trying to explain a play. Bottom line was that it wasn't about punishment, more so about discipline and being accountable for their actions. A team that listens and performs wins and hoists trophies. But they do it together, which is why as a team we often did pushups together as well, myself included. We won the championship three times during my five years on the coaching staff. It was a testament to the players who were willing to be coached, their dedication, and their hard work.

In the corporate world, leaders must do a lot of the same. Accountability is not the blame game. It's not for making sure people are blamed for their efforts, mistakes, etc. Accountability is ownership.

I've heard the below quote said by many people, in many forms. Every form still rings true.

> "Accountability is the glue that ties commitment to the result."
>
> — Bob Proctor

So as a leader you are looking for ownership in performance, effort, ethics, and behaviors, just to name a few. But those same things you are going to hold other people to are the same things you need to hold yourself to, maybe even higher. The second way accountability works is within leadership, and how leaders hold themselves accountable.

In the military, we always preach that we hold ourselves to a higher standard. That standard is higher than the average American, as we are willing to sign a check, payable up to our lives, for the values and safety this country holds so dear. In a sense, the military is the leader, willing

CHAPTER 17

to go above and beyond the norm in order to get the job done. They are willing to sacrifice a lot, get blamed for random things, and be judged.

I had plenty of people thank me for my service when I wore my uniform downtown. I typically tried not to, but when the wife says she needs ingredients for dinner, you pick them up on the way home. For every person who thanked me for my service and showed that appreciation, there were plenty of people who didn't. That's not to say people didn't appreciate it, just that they didn't say anything. Nothing wrong with that. But there were also people who didn't appreciate it and made that clear.

I had plenty of people give me ugly looks and even a few who called me names for wearing the uniform. In my opinion, it's disrespectful, but their opinion is their opinion. My point is this: you will never make everyone happy, yet you still have to get the job done.

Leaders must do the same. It doesn't matter what you wear to work that day. It could be a military uniform, scrubs from a hospital, a utility belt for a police officer, or a suit. If you lead people, you must be held to a higher standard, and you must hold yourself to a higher standard. Leadership is a thankless job, and at times will require you to fall on the sword. It is not a glorious thing by any means.

I've always approached accountable leadership like this: I'm going to hold you (the employee or follower) to a standard. That standard might be high, or it might be just in line with what you can handle, but I'm going to hold you to it. Then, I'm going to hold myself to it as well, plus another set of standards that I have for myself as your boss/manager or team leader. I will never ask you to do something I won't be willing to do myself, and I will hold myself to a higher standard than you at all times. Not because I want to show you up, but because if standards must be high, I must reach them as an example of great leadership.

The perspective of a prominent leader should, and always should, be that they are transparent in their efforts. I've screwed up just as many times as everyone else, and every single time it was hard to admit it. However, a transparent leader holds themselves accountable and isn't afraid of what it results in. You will absolutely gain more trust, respect, and understanding from the people you lead when you admit you are wrong rather than hiding it. When I held myself accountable and verbalized how I did so with my people, I could lead them at the highest of levels. When ego gets in the way, accountability fails.

RESPONSIBILITY

Of course, the most famous quote about responsibility is always the one from Spider-Man: "With great power comes great responsibility." It's catchy, and everybody loves saying it. It's probably the most famous quote from that trilogy of Spider-Man movies. Can you say another quote from any of the three Tobey Maguire Spider-Man movies? Nope, and I can't either. However, that quote is associated with the word *responsibility*, yet explains nothing about it.

What that quote is saying is that you have to be responsible all the time. When you are blessed with abilities or surrounded by people or things you are accountable for, you must be that level of responsible. You are responsible all the time, especially as a leader. But then you will have to be a higher level of responsible. In other words, you have to step your game up.

I think a better quote on responsibility defines the difference between accountability and responsibility, because often the two get mixed up. In reality, they are both very different.

> "Responsibility is accepting that you are the cause and the solution of the matter."
>
> — *Anonymous*

As with superheroes like Spider-Man, he's the cause and the solution. I don't remember what Avengers movie it was in, but at one point the characters discussed the fact that their collective abilities to be superheroes also invited fear and intimidation (don't quote me on that exactly!). In order to fight evil, they had to match that evil with an equal and greater power. That greater power invited intimidation. At that point they were the solution, as well as the cause. When a threat is created, it is then neutralized by an equal or greater threat. But, at the same time or even as a result, both threats then invite competition, inviting other threats to rise to the occasion. If you have something you want and someone stands in your way, you have two options. Run, or fight as hard as you can. If someone sees how hard you can fight and win, that then becomes the challenge, and you put a target on your back, even if you never intended to. When you have, or obtain, something others want, they will look to get it for themselves. Not everyone understands how to work for it, so instead, they will try and take the easiest path to success. They won't necessarily follow the rules or do things honestly; instead, they will do whatever it takes to obtain what you have. Instead of focusing on themselves, they will focus on you, ignoring their own accountability.

> "When you sit on the throne, there will always be someone looking to take the crown."
>
> — Anonymous

So why do accountability and responsibility get confused with each other? Why do they get mixed all the time? Well, it's simple. Accountability is being responsible. Think about that. Accountability is the act of being responsible. Responsibility is knowing what all you are accountable for and understanding your role in it. You are the cause of things, as well as the potential solution.

Responsibility is a heavy thing. The weight of the world could be on your shoulders, and that's a significant amount of pressure and added stress. Leaders have to balance everything they are responsible for, as the bigger the position of leadership, the more responsibility. Every time I took a new job it involved new responsibilities, whether those things were new processes or an increase in people. Each time was a challenge, and each time I had to learn how to balance it all. The best way to do that is to combine accountability with responsibility and turn it into delegation.

Delegation is a great tool for leaders *if* they understand how to use it correctly. The problem with people is they use delegation to free themselves up at the expense of making other people busy. I've worked for people who thought delegation was just part of leadership, and they delegated everything. They then thought holding other people accountable for their work was also their primary job, so when things went bad they had someone to blame.

One of the biggest lessons I ever learned was when I told my boss, "I delegated it and then they messed it up." He then turned to me and said, "I never relieved you of responsibility. I just told you to get it done. How you accomplished it was up to you, but at the end of the day, whether or not you delegated it, you are still responsible." I later learned the value of being able to delegate and also empower people. A few years after that, I had this same conversation with a young troop I was mentoring. He told me the same thing, and I explained it to him just how my supervisor explained it to me. You are still at fault. You are still responsible. The only difference is you added another layer of accountability.

HEAR THESE TRUTHS

The acronym AAR encompasses a lot of things. But for people looking to lead teams to further success, or new success, the understanding of these things is key. Progress isn't made without an understanding of how you got there, so an AAR is always worth your time. Listen, review, act, and execute.

"There is only one rule for being a good talker—learn to listen."

CHAPTER 18
PERFORMANCE

HERE'S THE TRUTH...

Performance is the best way to shut people up.

KEY PERFORMANCE INDICATORS (KPI), also known as performance metrics, analytics, and various other terms, measure company and even individual performance. They are important measurements of performance, displaying how a team or an individual does their job. We can use these in manufacturing and production, as well as in customer service and sales. KPIs have evolved as business and e-commerce have grown, and now all kinds of different metrics can be measured. If you dream it up, it probably can be measured somehow. Knowing your KPIs is important to nearly every manager who ever existed, but KPIs are not everything. There is much more to your organization than that.

> "You don't lead by hitting people over the head—
> that's assault, not leadership."
>
> — Dwight Eisenhower

I taught a class while on active duty for senior management that targeted young middle managers as they prepared to become brand-new senior-level managers. The class focused heavily on rules, regulations, and official guidance. It focused on measuring output, results, and performance as well. For every middle manager, this was important because it would be their bread and butter once they moved into senior management positions, as they would be responsible for the performance of the department. To say it was an enormous responsibility was an understatement, as some of these middle managers didn't even possess a formal college degree, let alone any kind of business degree. Not all who came through the course had degrees, but many did. Their formal education on how to run a business and a supply operation came from us. When you are dealing with millions of taxpayer dollars every single year, you have to know how to account for it, spend it, and justify it.

We used this program called Business Objects, which pulled information from our supply database and allowed us to generate reports, even custom reports. This program allowed for our middle-level managers to see and create reports that senior-level managers used in their daily management. We spent three days teaching this program. We could have just shown them how to pull up standardized reports or templates we created for them, but we wanted each student to understand the program and the depth of information that was out there. Why? Because KPIs aren't always about performance.

At the end of the three days each student would always be burnt out on the program, as they had to not only learn it, but then prove to use through a series of assignments that they could create the reports from scratch. Students always had fun using the program and getting creative with what they could generate, and over time we even incorporated some of their custom reports into the curriculum.

One day when we had just completed the third day of teaching Business Objects I had all my students print off their largest report. One at a time, they all went to the printer and printed off their biggest report. Once everyone had their report printed, I asked them to hold up their report, grab it with two hands, and rip it apart. I did this for every class after that for almost two years. Nine times out of ten there was dead silence in the room after I told them to rip it up. All that hard work and this guy just wants us to throw it away? Yep, and here's why.

Performance metrics aren't always about performance. We overanalyze things and get caught up in the numbers way too often. Managers use performance metrics to see results, but they forgot how they got those results in the first place. Leaders understand that performance metrics are only part of the equation, and that human performance is the other half.

CHAPTER 18

> "One of the biggest pitfalls for performance measurement is to measure the 'part' with ignorance of the 'whole.'"
>
> — Pearl Zhu

You should absolutely, positively, without a doubt be spending *just* as much time on human performance as you do on company performance. If you are not, then you are a manager, not a leader. Don't call yourself one, because you aren't one. Managers only care about company performance and the bottom line. Leaders care about all the above, including their most important asset: people.

Let me be clear, splitting it 50/50 is the minimum. The more you invest in people, the easier those KPIs will eventually become to analyze. The goal should be to have quick and simple discussions about company performance, ensuring you are hitting target goals and not finding any alarming errors. That stuff is all good, but it's not everything. Train people to do tasks and you will get results. Train people on how to be people, and you will get performance. There is a big, big difference.

I can teach someone how to do a job, but if they don't really like me as a manager, or their job for that matter, they will have a higher chance of doing a poor job.

> "You ain't done nothing if you've done it halfway."
>
> — Blake Shelton from his song, "Hell Right"

The above quote is actually from a Blake Shelton song. As a native of Oklahoma, I grew up listening to Garth Brooks, Toby Keith, and Reba McEntire. When Blake Shelton hit the scene, he was a big deal for us because he was closer to my age group. I met Blake on a cruise one time, that oddly enough my wife and I won on a radio show. I normally don't believe in those contests, but I gave in to her persistence and we filled out the application online. A few days later we won!

As Blake soared to stardom, we watched his career closely, as I'm a big fan and I love his music. He's also a super nice guy and very down to earth. In 2020, he had a song called "Hell Right" with Trace Adkins. There's a line in the chorus that says, "You ain't done nothing if you've done it halfway." The line is in regard to raising hell *right* and having a good time. If you are going to do it, do it right. It's a catchy line that really made me think. What have you really accomplished if you did something only fifty percent?

A saying that has probably worn out its own value is "Giving 110%." I've heard it so much that I stopped listening to it and taking that kind of advice. I'm not giving my 110% as that is 10% too much. Instead, I'm going to give my 100%—100% of the time.

In my professional career I've always lived by the mantra, "Work hard during work hours, and when work ends, it ends." If I work from seven to four, I'm *working* from seven to four. I'm putting in the effort and grating away at my job to get it done. I'm giving it 100% effort the entire time because when four o'clock hits, I'm done. I'm not working after that. Instead, I'm going home because I'm actually done. And I can say that in confidence because I'm not slacking off or doing things 50% during that time. I'm at my maximum performance and plan on maximizing my time. When I go home, I go home knowing I got my work done, it was good or better quality, and I have no regrets about my performance that day.

I do this for two reasons. First, because I'm only getting paid for those set hours, so why work more for free? And second, because when I'm done working, my shift switches over to other things, like my family. I work hard so that my family can do fun things and benefit from my hard work. I owe them my 100% attention when I'm with them. I don't want to be distracted with work or work-related things. I preached this concept to my staff and told them that was my policy. You work hard from nine to five and then go home. And once you are home, you are home. You are no longer at work, so don't work. Nothing we do is going to end the world tomorrow, so be with your families. I need you at 100% while you are at work, so clock out and go be with family, drink those beers, and recharge the batteries.

Performance in leadership is all about walking the walk after you've talked the talk. Don't put words into play without actions. At four p.m. on a Friday I walked around and sent people home. It wasn't negotiable. If you were in the middle of something, find a stopping point and leave. I explained to my staff that it was just as important to me they spent time with family, enjoyed life outside of work, and recharged the batteries, as it was accomplishing work-related business. When work because life, life no longer exists. People can't do that forever, not even the most dedicated entrepreneurs.

Elon Musk, Steve Jobs, Jeff Bezos, and Warren Buffett were all known to work long hours dedicating themselves to not just becoming wealthy, but also achieving massive amounts of success. Every single one of them has publicly spoken about taking time off in order to be themselves, enjoy life, and recharge the batteries. Elon Musk was known to sleep on the floor of his manufacturing plants while Tesla was growing. He spent hours upon hours at work ensuring he was around when a decision needed to be made, or just to show support for those who were working to make Tesla successful. But during his weekends or his free time, he spent it with his kids. He never missed an opportunity to do that. Donald Trump was the same way. It was reported that he slept about four hours every night before he became the president. The Trump name had a large reputation. He was the entrepreneur's entrepreneur. Rappers talked about him like he was a god. His name was one of the few that belonged in the same sentence as "rich."

He dedicated himself to his business, making Trump a household name, and eventually making his family billionaires. Like him or not, he was successful despite many failures, and he worked hard at it. But he also owned a resort and several golf clubs that he frequented, never shying away from taking some time off. Why? Because even the biggest names in success understand the importance of taking time for themselves and recharging.

This ideology goes both ways. You, as a leader, must take care of yourself. Yes, it will be necessary at times to be the first one at work and the last one to leave. It will be necessary for you to work harder than anyone else in the room yet achieve the same results. Yes, being a leader sucks at times and is very stressful. However, if that is so obvious, why won't you take it into consideration when planning your day, week, or month? A lot of employers give paid time off to employees for a reason. They want you to take a break! You are only your best version of yourself when you are rested and ready, which is what they hired you for, so take the time off.

Time off is something I learned early in my career. The military gives you thirty days a year time off, plus all federal holidays and commander-directed down days. So it really turns into almost fifty days off if you take all of it. I routinely just took off the federal holidays and mandated down days, rarely taking off any of my thirty days. I spent a ton of time at work, depending on my wife to keep the house running. I turned my life into work, and my life became fragile. It was a huge mistake, and I regret not spending more time at home.

My philosophy now is to monitor my staff and their time-off balances. My first priority as a leader is them and their families. It's family first, mission second. Or as a first sergeant once told me, "Family First, Mission Always." People will perform at their optimum level when they feel optimal. It's simple. Take care of the little things and pave the way for optimal performance. You as a leader are not there to make them perform; rather, you are there to support them in performing.

"Excellence is doing ordinary things, extraordinarily well."

— John W. Gardne

CHAPTER 19
VULNERABILITY

HERE'S THE TRUTH...

People hide vulnerability because they fear being wrong or looking weak.

VULNERABILITY IS A HARD TOPIC to discuss. Being vulnerable is even harder, as you literally have to expose yourself, often in your weakest form. When vulnerable you are just that, vulnerable. People associate being vulnerable with weakness, and they prefer to be defensive rather than open to attack.

I've mentioned this previously, but as humans we are naturally defensive. Our brains automatically go into preservation mode and set up defenses when vulnerable to an attack. It doesn't matter if the attack appears to be mental or physical—our brains automatically do it. We do it to protect ourselves as well as others.

Ever have someone stick out their arm over you while driving for fear that you might get into a wreck? Most people my age or older understand that. The driver sticks out their arm over you, the passenger, hoping their arm will protect you in the event of an accident. In reality, the arm won't do anything. The arm will break and maybe stop some of the forward momentum of the passenger during an accident. It's almost a useless thing to do, especially now with passenger airbags. I imagine your arm will only fly around and probably shoot right back into the passenger because of the airbag deploying. I'm no expert in physics or vehicle safety, but I think I can accurately state that sticking your arm out is useless.

Now, have I done it plenty of times out of instinct? Sure, it's of course as stated... instinct. It's instinct because it's a natural defensive response during a threatening moment. We naturally protect what we feel is vulnerable. Some people do it more than others, while others don't fear nearly as much. Bravery is the counter word to vulnerability. My point is this: we naturally aren't vulnerable. As leaders, this is something we have to break.

Being vulnerable as a leader is not about going to one extreme or the other. It's about balance. You've got to know when to be vulnerable and when to be the tough guy. You've got to know when it's okay to be wrong, and when it's okay to be right. How you react in both situations says a lot about your character.

The below quote describes vulnerability perfectly. It's by Brené Brown. Brené is a professor, author, and podcast host hailing from the great state of Texas. She focuses heavily on leadership and on being courageous. Although I don't agree with everything she has to say, I love her insight and perspective. She has dropped some gems about leadership and courage that have really resonated with me.

> "Vulnerability is not weakness; it's our most accurate measure of courage."
>
> — Brené Brown

Being vulnerable is a tough thing to do. As the quote above states, it's not a weakness. Being vulnerable is, in a way, letting our guard down, but in doing that we also open ourselves up to the test of bravery and courage. When we let down our defenses, we open ourselves up to attack, or to be attacked. So vulnerability is in fact a test of courage and bravery. Opening up to being vulnerable means we very well could be hurt by something, and we are standing up, willing to let that happen for the greater good of things. I'm not ashamed at all to admit some things I've been vulnerable to, both professionally and personally. A friend of mine, Carl Shawn Watkins, is a vulnerability master. He coaches leaders of all types in the art of mastering vulnerability, and I'm honored that he contributed this quote to my book. It's one I want you to remember throughout this chapter.

CHAPTER 19

> "A successful man lays his foundation with the bricks that others have thrown at him..."
>
> — *Carl Shawn Watkins*

When I ran the medical warehouse at the large army hospital in San Antonio, I was one of the few Air Force guys within the supply operation. Military members from the army and civilians in the army surrounded me. Most of them had spent plenty of time with the army and were not familiar with the Air Force. But that wasn't the challenge. The challenge was for me.

I had worked with the Army before, but in a coworker-type capacity. We functioned together to get a specific job done, one that had a common interest and shared a lot of the same language. This time I found myself in a leadership role, supervising more army personnel than Air Force. I had a steep hill to climb and was very clearly out of my comfort zone. I had to learn a whole new language and method of doing things. The army had rules regarding how to manage and supervise their civilians, which differed from how the Air Force did some things. Not to mention, for the first time in my working career, I had to deal with a union.

I don't know if you've ever dealt with a union, or employees who knew they were protected under a union, but it was maybe the biggest and most frustrating challenge of my career. To put it into perspective, I had a bunch of civilians who couldn't agree on what we played on the radio. That's right. We couldn't agree on a radio station to play on the radio, five days out of the week. Even after discussions about what to play on what days just so everyone could get their preferences, and to make it fair, we as a team still couldn't decide. So as the boss I just decided to stop the fighting, and I removed the radio. And in came the union.

Apparently, you just can't do that. The employees then argued that their ability to listen to music and the news via the radio was taken away by me, leaving out that they argued about that same radio. So, at first they fought about what to listen to and couldn't agree on anything, but then they all agreed to hate me because I took away what they were arguing about. My solution actually caused a new problem. It was a confusing time.

> "The wisest of people in this world are those that can admit when they are wrong."
>
> — *Anonymous*

I was wrong. I thought taking decisive action would end the issues and the childish behavior. I was wrong. I ended up looking like an idiot and having to apologize. It was tough, because as I looked into the eyes of those employees, I could tell how much they loved that I was apologizing and looking stupid. And I hated every minute of it. But it taught me a big lesson in admitting I was wrong. Because unlike them, I could admit it. Now I had nothing to hide, no reason to wear protection to defend myself. I was exposed, attacked, and recovered. It was likely the best thing I could have done. Now I was a leader who had experienced not only being wrong, but a little public humiliation, something none of them were willing to do.

The fight continued until I finally one day discovered who the owner was, and they claimed to hate the fighting and wanted to just take their radio back home. I approved, and the next day the radio was gone. Someone tried to file another complaint on me with the union, to which I responded that the original owner of the radio decided to take it back home as it was their own personal property. Nothing I could do about that.

That lesson taught me a lot about vulnerability. Sometimes you are just out of your element, out of your comfort zone, and are very vulnerable to being attacked. You want to put up defenses and take action to stop the problem or protect yourself, but that doesn't always work. In my case it actually made things worse, and I spent nearly two weeks dealing with the local union officials while they agreed with the problem I was having but stood by their represented employees. There was no way for me to win, and I felt like a loser. I was very vulnerable at that time because that wasn't my only issue.

I was also having issues with a fellow military member who thought he could treat me like dirt and push me around. He anointed himself as the boss and took charge when he didn't need to. Most of the unit didn't like him and didn't respect him. I didn't either, but I did the right thing as a leader and tried my hardest to show him respect and work with him. It was tough, and we fought a ton. He was the kind of guy to embarrass you in front of your people just to try and show off his power. Multiple times he waited for me to come in to work just so he could find something to complain about. He was toxic and understood how vulnerable I was in the current situation. He tried his hardest to break me and did a few times. I, however, sucked it up and just made sure I took care of my troops and staff who worked for me.

Later on, we had a meeting with some of our senior leadership. I raised some of my concerns and brought his actions to the table. They were fully aware of these things, and as I explained the situation and how I wanted to work with him, but how he made that hard to do, he simply excused his actions, blaming my lack of leadership. The meeting was fairly unsuccessful, and I left feeling as if my voice wasn't really heard. Turns out it was, and a few months later this guy was actually transferred to a new unit, where he did the same things, and was eventually kicked out of the army. He invested over fifteen years of his life in the army, only to be kicked out because of his ego. He was the typical egocentric asshole, and it got in the way. He never saw his potential to be vulnerable and grow, and it cost him his career. He upset the wrong people for far too long, thinking he was untouchable. Well, he eventually met his match and got sent home.

In leadership, we have to learn how to be vulnerable, understanding that it isn't a bad thing. When people see you as vulnerable, they see you as human, not an indestructible force. Ideally, you want your followers to see you as a leader, someone who can kick ass and take names, while being able to connect with them at all different kinds of levels. Plus, you want to be seen as someone who can make mistakes and be vulnerable to attacks. Why? Again, because it makes you human.

Part of being vulnerable is also setting the tone for the workplace. Great leaders and great bosses set the tone and know that their actions and language have a large impact. If you are a mistake-free, egocentric, expecting-perfection-type of leader or boss, how do you think your team will react? The likelihood of them being afraid of failure, avoiding mistakes, and seeking perfection is very high. However, seeking all those things is actually a recipe for disaster. If you openly admit to a mistake, or a wrong decision, that reveals your human side. It lets everyone around you know that mistakes happen even to the best of us. Running from mistakes will only lead to creating more mistakes. Rather, embracing the fact that they happen, despite trying to keep them from happening, will actually prevent future mistakes. It's better to learn a lesson from a mistake than to run from the mistake in the first place.

Yes, avoidance will help, but it's not a good preventative practice. Working to avoid mistakes only deters you from the primary reason to work in the first place. As a worker, if I'm more focused on being error-free so that I don't have to be vulnerable, I'm not focused on the task at hand. Me personally, as a leader, I want my people to focus on quality with the understanding that nothing will be perfect. Mistakes will happen, and although I want them to work hard to keep them from happening, when they do happen we talk about them and learn from it. We as a team are vulnerable.

Vulnerability is actually the key to better relationships. Instead of competing against each other on who can be the best, mistake free human, you are letting your guard down and showing the real you. Being safe with the way you act, the way you dress, and the way you operate is just fine, but it's no real projection of you. Be a leader and be vulnerable, showing the side of you that will connect on a human level with the people you lead. Those connections will pay big dividends down the road.

I struggled to find the right quote to end this chapter. I searched for days and only found quotes about love, strength, and mushy stuff. None of them hit me like the one below.

"The only way to patch a vulnerability is by exposing it first."

— Elliot Anderson

CHAPTER 20
FLEXIBILITY

HERE'S THE TRUTH...
The key to a successful culture is flexibility.

I AM NOT A physically flexible person. My body just doesn't bend very well. I wish it could because I bet it would make me feel so much better. However, I understand the importance of flexibility. Flexibility by definition is the quality of bending easily without breaking. Keep that in mind as we discuss this section, as we focus on making progress in this part of the algorithm. You will not make the progress you want to make without being flexible. Progress is not about forcing results, as much as it is about embracing the results that come and improving on them.

> "Be clear about your goal, but be flexible about the process of achieving it."
>
> — *Brian Tracy*

Flexibility is one of those things that people can see immediately. It's the difference between a stubborn boss and a flexible one. Exemplary leaders understand that being flexible pays dividends. They also understand that flexibility is a tool, and it shouldn't be taken advantage of. Sometimes you have to stand tall or take a firm position. Nothing wrong with that. But being flexible in certain scenarios or situations can actually yield more results than you think.

We don't have a lot of flexibility in society anymore. Our political system has created a society that either believes they are right or wrong. If you are on the wrong side, you are brushed to the side and ignored. If you are right, you ignore any other voices around you and stick to what you think is right. It's created a world where we can't be flexible, let alone compromise. This hard stance on right versus wrong doesn't work, as is obvious by the lack of actual progress in politics and the constant changing of political party in Washington. Leadership should be stable, but willing to be flexible in its actions and to compromise when it makes sense to compromise. Common sense might not be that common (especially in politics) but should always prevail in leadership.

The act of being flexible is a mental process, a psychological connection to people. It affects everything from morale to dynamics to understanding to culture. A boss who is a strict nine-to-five worker and expects everyone to be perfectly on time and not leave until the clock strikes five is not very flexible. He probably runs a tight ship and expects a mistake-free culture, a likely unrealistic expectation. There are some exceptions. Jobs that are dangerous in nature, or around heavy machinery, for example. Mistake-free could save a life. However, there is a difference between mistake-free expectations and just being disciplined in specific protocols to achieve the same result.

The boss or manager who yells at you for being five minutes late is not flexible. Instead, they are taking a hard stance on the matter of timeliness, ignoring anything else with the matter. If that report is due today at noon, but you know that turning it in by the end of the day would allow for a better product and the boss says no despite your reasoning, that boss or manager might not be very flexible. Of course, there are tight deadlines and sometimes deadlines are set for specific reasons, but reasoning should be part of the process.

I've listened plenty of times when asked for an extension. I look at it as being flexible. I want to hear why an extension is being requested, and I also want to see the work completed so far. It's a balance. I get to grant an extension, and further understand why one was being asked for. Plus, I get to see a sneak peek at the progress. I've had workers before who asked for an extension because they blew something off and were short on time. Extension granted but I want to see the progress so far. Turns out there was no progress because it was a failure on their part to schedule and plan. And that's a different conversation.

But if someone can verbalize to you the plan, the progress so far, and the need for an extension, as a leader, I can get behind that. I have no problem granting an extension, and even explaining to someone above me why it's important. At that point I know you are dedicated to the job, and the task will only be a better product with additional time to complete it. That I can be flexible with.

I can also be flexible with the work schedule. If you have a flat tire and are going to be late, call me. Let me know. If I can come help I will. If not I'll be understanding and flexible. Realistically, life gets in the way. People have to live their lives and sometimes that's hard to do when the unexpected occurs. You seriously can't expect a single mother to take care of three kids and be on time every single day. Cut her some slack and the reduced stress might actually allow her to work more efficiently. It may be my personality, or my combination of working with military, but I'm more concerned with taking care of people than the clock. I've had military spouses work for me while their spouse was deployed. They are left with running the house, taking care of kids, and working a full-time job with minimal days off. So, you need to shift your schedule around to take little Johnny to the doctor? Great, let's talk about it. My ego is not so big that I can't be flexible. That's ridiculous.

It's amazing what shrugging off five minutes can do for morale. Should it happen consistently? No, of course not. Should you still address the issue? Yes, absolutely. But there is a commonsense approach to doing so. Acknowledging with the individual that they were late is one thing, as you intend to reinforce the expectations while understanding mistakes happen. But to yell, scream, and demean someone over five minutes? You can potentially do a lot of damage, and for what? If that employee is already stressed and is running late, and you yell at them over five minutes, you really could ruin their entire day. Now what performance are you going to get out of them?

Instead, a simple, "Hey, noticed you were late today—everything okay?" question might elicit a better response while acknowledging the tardiness. This kind of initiation allows for you, as the leader, to address the issue while maintaining a personal connection with the issue. Now they can see that you genuinely care and want to make sure everything is okay. People who are happy with their job are more likely to work harder, be happier, and come to work loyal. In the long run you are going to get more than five minutes of performance out of them by handling the situation differently.

By being flexible and understanding the situation, I can actually get more performance out of this employee by helping relieve some of their stress. I'm flexible in this situation, and other similar situations because doing things by the book all the time will crush morale. I've seen it firsthand. The more I was flexible without totally breaking the rules, the more I got out of my team. Every. Single. Time. The rules are made to give us parameters to operate within. They are not perfect guidelines for every scenario. Outstanding leaders understand those rules can bend without breaking and will take a gamble on what is right.

> "The little things pay way more dividends than gambling on the big things."

These are all just little things, but worth it in the end. The little things add up and turn into higher morale and motivation. How much time are you going to spend harping on these little things compared to how much value you get out of them being five minutes late? How many tasks can you complete in five minutes? Not very many, so why waste time dealing with it?

Now this isn't to say that you shouldn't be light on the rules. If problems become consistent, they have to be addressed. Rules cannot be broken over and over again without a consequence, no matter how well people perform. But knowing when to lower the hammer and when to shrug it off is an artform, one that you have to judge for yourself. But be fair, be prepared, and hold everyone accountable. Being flexible can show strength, understanding, and accountability without appearing weak.

The quicker leaders understand things come up, the quicker they'll realize being flexible is actually more productive and efficient than the alternative. I've mentioned it before in this book, but it's worth mentioning again. We had this saying in the Air Force: "Flexibility is the key to airpower." The better understanding we have of flexibility, the more air-dominating we can be. And maintaining air dominance around the world was a big priority. You can't maintain your status as the best Air Force in the world by being stubborn and sticking to the plans perfectly. It just won't work. And neither will being a leader while working in the same manner.

I've had a boss before that busted me every time I was late. If I tried to call he wouldn't answer, so I could never give him a head's up. But he'd always be looking for me when I showed up. He was never understanding and always gave me a bunch of grief. I hated him. Turns out he was just an asshole and treated everyone like that. And everybody else hated him too. The position I was in had high turnover, and I was like the fifth or sixth employee they had hired in, like, six months. Nobody lasted very long because of this guy. He wasn't understanding, wasn't patient, and wasn't flexible. He not only caused his own stress, but he also created stress for others. For no reason at all. He didn't understand that true leadership is not about you; it's about others.

I can't stress the importance of flexibility. In my experience, some of the best leaders knew the importance of being flexible. Also, in my personal experience, flexibility helped me to be a better leader. When I needed to bend, I would bend. No sense in taking a tough stance because your ego won't let you bend. I gained way more progress when I was flexible. And when people took advantage of my flexibility, I let them know. The disappointment alone was enough to make them rethink their decision. I didn't have to suspend, demote, or degrade anybody.

The old saying, "You'll catch more flies with honey than you will with vinegar," rings true here. Flexibility understands that. Leaders understand that. Sometimes you just can't be flexible. Trust me, I've been there myself. Those are the times when it's appropriate to stand your ground or stick to a firm deadline. Nothing wrong with that. But when you have the opportunity to be flexible, be flexible to the appropriate level. It will be worth it in the end. In my career, I've spent very little time on the "red carpet" in front of my boss explaining my actions when it involved taking care of my team. And the times I did, I willingly admitted I bent the rules in order to do right by my staff. I owned it, because leaders own their decisions regardless of outcome.

Never be afraid to be flexible—it's one of your greatest tools.

> "Stay committed to your decisions. But stay flexible in your approach."
>
> — Tony Robbins

CHAPTER 21
INNOVATE AND MOTIVATE

HERE'S THE TRUTH...

People slap the word *innovative* in front of stolen or meaningless ideas. *Motivation* has become a lazy man's word.

UNFORTUNATELY, IN TODAY'S SOCIETY, we overuse some words and phrases to the point that they no longer mean anything. It's hard to feel motivated by something when you've heard it a million times. It's also hard to innovate when environments aren't optimized for creativity.

I took special care in selecting the quotes for this book. Quotes are a dime a dozen today, and I have my own massive collection of them. I specifically picked quotes and words that I hadn't really seen before, or that had a special purpose in my leadership journey. I wanted them all, and the ones in this chapter in particular, to be top-notch. After all, I've heard way too many people overuse and incorrectly speak about innovation and motivation.

To be fair, I'm biased toward the words *innovate* and *innovative* because the Air Force used them so much they had to rename their innovation cells to spark cells. I've heard those words so many damn times it's not even funny. The problem with both of those words is that people don't use them in the proper context. *Innovate* used to mean testing the boundaries of the imagination and seeing if the idea could work. We often reserved it for crazy ideas, those types of ideas that seemed too good to be true. Things that nobody could fathom at all, yet someone attempted to do. Now it's used as a way to describe something that really isn't all that creative.

A friend of mine told me that the concept for this book was innovative. I laughed. Although I appreciated the compliment and the high praise, my explanation to him was simple: this isn't anything that hasn't been thought of before. I just finally put my own words and thoughts into it. I simply took a phrase and injected my own specific details into it. Algorithms have been used before. I just manipulated the concept to fit my perspective.

The same can go for other authors and big thinkers. Simon Sinek comes to mind. When he did his Ted Talk on "Find Your Why," it took some time to get popular. I'm not taking anything away from him at all, as eventually his Ted Talk blew up, but nothing he was saying was new. What Simon did, and did well, was put his spin on it. He formed his words to explain to the world how *he* saw "why," and what it meant to him. His perspective gave the audience plenty to think about, and sometimes a fresh perspective is more motivating than anything else. As he explained his perspective on "why," it was new, impactful, and creative. The basic principles of it were nothing really new, but his unique understanding and perspective was. The book he wrote on it was so impactful I read it twice. And his other book, *Leaders Eat Last*, was an outstanding read, as I also read it twice. I've gifted it to many people in my career and will continue to gift it (alongside my book!).

Can you imagine being there when Edison brought up the idea of a light bulb? I bet those people thought he was crazy. You are going to run an electrical current through wires into a glass bulb with more wires and it will glow?

Insanity, but true innovation. He created something completely new. Electricity and the lightbulb didn't exist before then. The idea was truly groundbreaking, and it changed our lives forever.

I bet people felt the same way when Elon Musk said he would design all electric cars that were stylish, could perform, and would implement technology that no other car manufacturer was willing to include. Although he didn't found Tesla, he provided funding in the early days and took over as CEO in 2008. In 2008 we were in Iraq and Afghanistan fighting terrorists with outdated vehicles and equipment. Meanwhile, Musk was busy developing an all-electric car in a market dominated by large trucks and poor gas mileage. This wasn't the first attempt at an electric car by any means, but what Musk would do to the auto industry was truly disruptive, and forcefully innovative. Now today, every auto manufacturer is working on all electric technology for their vehicles.

But he stuck with it, proclaiming he was going to deliver a mildly affordable, all-electric car, with high-end features, and a futuristic outlook. Today, Tesla is insanely popular and capturing more and more automotive market share daily. Tesla also forced the hand of innovation, and instead of hybrid electric cars, just about everyone is developing their own all-electric technology.

Ten years ago, all-electric cars sounded insane, let alone a large vehicle being electric. Ford Motor Company is designing an all-electric version of their flagship truck, the F-150, which will haul and get decent mileage on nothing but electricity. Large transportation companies are looking for all-electric options too, and companies are designing options for long-distance transportation. One day we just might see an all-electric semi-truck hauling your next Amazon Prime package across state lines, with a solar panel roof constantly recharging the one-ton battery underneath it.

You know what else sounded insane? Carrying around several hundred songs in your pocket in an era dominated by CDs. I remember the large CD case I had in my car. It held several hundred CDs. If I needed to change the song, I had to switch out the CD. It was the best option we had, and you could hold thousands of songs in that CD case. For one company, that CD case was bulky and unnecessary.

Apple said they were going to put thousands of songs on a small device that could fit in your pocket, in a time when CDs holding only probably twenty songs reigned supreme. It changed the nature of how we listened to music forever, and then Apple smashed a phone, iPod, email, calendar, and just about everything else under the sun into a device called the iPhone. Their desires for innovation were so lofty that they literally built an App Store so other people could develop apps for consumers to download. As of 2020, the Apple App Store had nearly two billion apps available for download. That's just the Apple store. Our lives haven't been the same since. My point is this: don't be afraid of innovation. All ideas sound crazy until they are not.

> "It's only a crazy dream until you do it."
>
> — Serena Williams

Technology has been innovating for decades now, with no end in sight. The B-2 stealth bomber used by the Air Force was designed in the 60s and 70s. The best we could drive back then was eight-cylinder cars that today we call muscle cars. Big-block engines with horrible gas mileage.

Meanwhile, in a development lab, people were designing a triangular-shaped aircraft that could beat radar detection.

The F-22 Raptor, the most advanced and deadly fighter aircraft in the world today, was developed in the 80s. Let me say that again... a secret stealth aircraft that went into service after the year 2000 was designed in the 80s. We still listened to cassette tapes and used VCRs in the 80s. Digital media wasn't a thing yet, and the only people who had computers were businesses, and not all of them. Computers weren't in every home yet and wouldn't be for a while. Yet, in a development lab somewhere, the next generation fighter jet was going to not only dominate the air, but also be invisible.

I'm sure if you would have asked someone in the 80s what they thought of an advanced aircraft that couldn't been seen by radar, had highly sophisticated avionics and computer systems, and thrust technology unlike anything we've ever seen, they wouldn't respond with anything other than a laugh. Stealth technology and being invisible were for movies and comic books, not military planes. But in April 1997 the B-2 Spirit stealth bomber was introduced to the world. Eight years later in December 2005, the world was introduced to the F-22 Raptor, the superior fighter jet of any military force, and yet again, with minimal radar signature. All that technology was developed decades before the introduction.

Apple was started in the 80s as well, out of a garage. Now they are one of the largest and most influential companies in the world (and maybe history). The introductions they've made to consumers have changed their lives, and therefore, changed the world. How we live, work, and play were all influenced by companies like Apple. Pushing innovation when people thought it was insane. True innovation has been happening for decades. The motivation to do so has introduced us to some fantastic people from all around the world. Brilliant minds who didn't do things the conventional way. Innovation succeeds from motivated minds.

Something I always made sure I did as a leader was motivate—and motivate to innovate. At one point I was a huge rule-follower. I didn't want to do anything outside of what the rules of the military told me I could do. I never questioned policy or guidance. At least, until I started supervising people and I had to view things from both a leader and worker perspective. Then I realized it's not so easy to just follow directions when it doesn't work in your favor.

My policy ever since that day was to do things according to the book, following the rules. If we as a team discovered it wouldn't work, or wasn't optimal, we discussed and developed a process to make it work.

It wasn't breaking the rules, but it was getting the job done the most efficient way possible.

Sometimes rules and regulations are drafted to encompass everything for everybody. The military often does that so that an entire force can have proper guidance. However, guidance for me at my base didn't always work for someone else at another base. So, we try to make it work and if it doesn't, we find a legal and ethical way to make it work. Then, as we've discussed before, we have an After Action Review to document our new process. I'm a firm believer in never forcing a square peg into a round hole, so if we can innovate and be creative, let's do it.

INNOVATION

As a leader, you should never be afraid to innovate or be afraid of innovation. Groundbreaking thoughts, ideas, and processes are the only way to keep up in today's world. Tomorrow a new iPhone will be released, followed by new software to run it and a competitor right on their heels. And that's just for a cell phone. There're thousands of other products doing the exact same thing. Today, you simply can't be afraid of innovation and creativity.

Innovation as a word, however, has become a very inflated term. It's been overused for a while now and substituted often. In my opinion, innovation has been used in situations where creativity doesn't exist. It's become a word to use when there are no other solutions, and nobody can come up with a creative idea. It's lost its value, and mainly because we've devalued it.

Webster's Dictionary defines innovate as:

innovate (verb)
1. to introduce as or as if new
2. to effect a change in

innovation (noun)
1. a new idea, method, or device
2. the introduction of something new

Bringing new ideas to the table is what innovation is about. Finding new ways of doing things, developing new thoughts, ideas, and even devices was and is still what innovation is all about. In other words, not doing the norm and finding a new norm is what innovation is.

So why an entire chapter dedicated to innovation and what the hell does it have to do with leadership? Well, *first,* leadership should never be afraid to innovate. *Second,* leadership should understand innovation.

Some of the great leaders of our world today unconditionally understood innovation. They also understood that in order to be an innovative company, they must have innovative leadership. Elon Musk, Steve Jobs, Jeff Bezos, and many others didn't become familiar names by just simply running effective companies. You'd never have heard about Tesla if they were making gasoline-powered cars just like GM, Ford, and all the others. Tesla would get lost in the shuffle and would probably be irrelevant today. No, you've heard of Tesla because Elon Musk is an innovator. He wants to push the envelope of creativity and business. He's fully embraced innovation, with some people even comparing him to a modern-day Tony Stark.

We could say the same of Tim Cook. Tim took over Apple when the late Steve Jobs passed away. There was some uncertainty when the innovative mind of Steve Jobs was laid to rest. Would Apple be the company Jobs pushed it to be? Would they continue to break barriers and blow our minds? The answer was a firm, "Yes." And Tim Cook delivered on the innovation. And that's because he understood the culture that Apple had, the culture that flourished under Jobs, and what he had to do to continue that culture.

Prominent leaders understand that innovation doesn't have to come from them. These leaders understand that fostering a culture of creative thinking will create innovative opportunities. And if you want to be innovative, you have to have your employees busy innovating.

I read a book called *Creative Selection* by Ken Kocienda. It was about his time at Apple during the creation of the iPhone and iPad. Ken was a leader and designer behind the framework for the iPhone keypad. Although the iPhones we use today are not exactly his design anymore, he was the guy behind figuring out how to have a keyboard on a phone without using physical keys. Ken worked several levels below Steve Jobs. He reported to half a dozen other people, who all reported to Steve Jobs. Innovation started at Ken's level, not Steve's. Steve Jobs knew innovation when he saw it and supported it.

I, for one, as a leader, want to make not only my job easier, but my team's job as well. How do you do that? Encourage Innovation! Tell your people that if they have a better way of doing business to bring it to the table for discussion. Got a good idea? Let's talk! Have monthly meetings that are strictly for discussing how things are going.

CHAPTER 21

No agenda, just get your team talking about how the job and projects are being done.

As a leader, I want my team to feel comfortable enough to tell me when something sucks. I flat-out want to know. If the process is taking extra time and creating extra work for no reason at all, I want to know that. I also want to analyze it and find out why. I also want to create a culture within my team that gets each member to speak up, tell the truth, and find solutions.

I think the single most important thing I taught my troops when I was on active duty was to think for themselves. As a supervisor my job was to be the boss, the identified leader of the team. But also, I had a job to mold and teach my replacements. The people who worked for me one day would be in my shoes, and hopefully in bigger shoes after that. So when one of my troops brought me a complaint or a problem, I thanked them for bringing it to my attention and then asked them, "What would you do?" or "How do we fix it?" Not because I'm lazy and don't want to figure it out myself, but because I understood the importance of fostering creative thinking within the ranks.

One person can't be the only designated person to come up with solutions and ideas. It just won't work. As a supervisor I had enough things to do, let alone deal with every problem and find every solution. But you know who has solutions? The people working in the trenches. I made it a point to ask them what they thought of the problem or complaint when they brought it to me. I empowered them to come up with a solution, a new idea, or change. Because change is easier when people buy-in, and innovation is easier when everyone is trying.

No ideas were ever off the table. Everything was considered, discussed, and analyzed. No such thing as a stupid idea; nothing is a waste of time. You want to foster new and fresh ideas? That's how you do it. Yes, you are the boss with most likely the final say. But that doesn't mean you can't get input from the team. After all, they are going to know best how to fix the issues that THEY are dealing with. If you can't get them to talk and discuss the basic problems in the workplace, how do you expect them to go steps further and innovate?

People naturally want to do things quicker, so they will cut corners. Those corner-cutters may seem lazy, but have you really reviewed why they are cutting those corners? Or are you just annoyed by the fact that they are cutting corners in the first place? Is it really laziness or is there a better way of doing something altogether? As a leader, you should be finding that out.

HEAR THESE TRUTHS

MOTIVATION

Now, let's talk about *motivation*. Simply put, you can't innovate if you aren't motivated. If I have no reason to innovate, then why would I waste my time? Am I supposed to innovate for the sake of innovating? Or do I have a reason, an outside influence, or maybe even a reward for innovating? What is the driving motivator?

Webster's Dictionary defines motivation as:

motivation (noun)
1. a motivating force, stimulus, or influence

It motivated Steve Jobs to create a computer, something different from what was already on the market. It wasn't a simple task, and they fired him from Apple, and he also left the company several times. In order to achieve his goal, he stayed motivated. Apple wasn't even a household name until the early 2000s. Jobs created Macintosh in his garage in the 80s. It took over 20 years of dedication, small successes, and failures before the iPod changed our lives. Motivation was the driving force behind changing the world for Steve Jobs.

Motivation can be a difficult thing to master, as everyone has their own motivating factors. For me, I just love to lead people. If I didn't have bills to pay, I'd do it for free. But, I have bills to pay and other people who rely on me, which is my primary motivator. I want to take care of my family and have financial freedom, and so do your team members.

My secondary motivator is the pleasure I get in taking care of people and leading them to doing great things. I have to prioritize money as number one, but only because I have to. If not, the family would be in a world of hurt. I know and understand this and can explain it to my boss if needed. But how do you get down to that level of detail with your team?

First, establish a rapport with them. The connections you make will open doors to further communication. You have to remember that people aren't necessarily going to trust you immediately. Some people will, but others will be reserved. For every one person you have that opens up to you quickly, I bet you have at least three that won't. It's easy to lead the ones who are open with you but leading the ones who aren't is the challenge.

Finding out what motivates people doesn't have to be difficult. It can be difficult, but it doesn't have to be. It can be little things. The issue with searching is that we are often looking for something, which jades our vision and in turn keeps us from seeing the obvious. I mentioned this earlier when talking about hearing the truth. You can't be looking for something; you have to be observing everything and watching for clues and details. Sometimes what motivates people will sit right out in the open, staring them in the face.

I'll provide you an example, going back to my warehouse days with the army. When I first took the job, the chief complaint from my staff was that they were the last section in the entire division to get funding. They rarely had what they needed, never even got a chance to request it, and equipment was old and failing. Upon doing some research I found out that the previous guy in charge didn't put a priority on those things, and when funding was available, he never jumped on it.

So I went to my boss and asked for funding. Of course, there wasn't any available, but she told me the date to come back and see her about it again. I marked that date on my calendar and was in her office first thing when that day arrived. In turn, ours was the first section to receive funding. I took that opportunity to ask about requesting larger funding for new equipment and other needs. I learned the process that day and made it one of my top priorities.

In the first six months that I was in charge, we got plenty of funding to buy what we needed. Didn't have much to buy what I wanted, but we got what we needed, and I rationed it. It was a big change, and I could see how it motivated the staff. They finally received at least some of the things they needed to do their jobs, despite being grumpy about doing it.

Small wins!

However, I didn't stop there. I tasked one of my junior members to help me with bigger procurement packages. This meant new equipment, new computers and printers, and some nice-to-have items. It took several months of hard work, justification, and pleading with leadership, but I got it. We received new pallet jacks, everybody got a new utility knife, new pens, markers, and office products, as well as brand new chairs, desks, and safety equipment. For them it felt like Christmas almost every day for nearly a month. For me it was just part of doing my job and doing right by them. I could see their loyalty to me rise, as well as their daily motivation. Their faith in me had increased, and I could hold them more accountable.

In this situation, it was all about finding those motivating factors. I simply observed and found out what basic motivator was missing. For them it was just simply the supplies they needed to do their job and feel as if the organization was investing in them. I invested in them, and in turn we became a better-performing section. It's a very generalized motivator, but it is one, nonetheless.

Bigger motivators like that are options you can execute quickly, with quick results. As leaders, they might seem like small things, but we must remember that small things to us are big things to others. Don't underestimate those things or fail to put value to them.

"There is no greater danger than underestimating your opponent."

— Lao Tzu

Motivation is a driving force behind human behavior. It gives people purpose and a desire to continue toward goals, both personal and professional.

Finding the motivators within your team can be a challenge. There's no question about it. Some people are simple and just want to do their job and go home, ensuring that check hits the bank account every two weeks. They do great work, keep to themselves, and that work environment keeps them happy and, frankly, motivates them to come back tomorrow and do it all over again. That process is not broken, so leaders don't attempt to fix it.

Some people, however, want bigger things. That's what motivates them. They want to learn, grow, and seek promotions. Cash rewards and time off motivate others. Some people want to get extremely rich. Others love their job because they are passionate about it. And lastly, some people do their job because it fuels their hobbies, which are extremely important to them.

For me, I am also motivated to do my job because it funds my creative ventures. It allows me to do my writing, develop other ideas, and eventually host a podcast. I don't mind my job at all, but it is a formality.

I challenge all leaders to find out what motivates your staff and team. Sometimes it boils down to just flat-out asking. During feedback sessions, I used to ask the question, "What motivates you?" I often got a blank stare or generalized answers, but the more I asked it the more specific the answers became. Especially when I acted on those answers.

The staff eventually understood that what they expressed to me didn't fall on deaf ears, and I took it seriously. Obviously, I couldn't make everything happen, but I tried to make some things happen that would impact them.

Understanding motivators and motivation will lead to better innovation, better performance, and better cohesion. Not everyone

CHAPTER 21

comes to work just for the dollar. People do come to work for many other reasons. I challenge every leader to find out what those things are and use them to your advantage. If we can't motivate, how are we supposed to innovate? And without motivation, how do we understand purpose? If we don't understand purpose, why are we even here?

> "We are here to put a dent in the universe.
> Otherwise, why else even be here?"
>
> — *Steve Jobs*

CHAPTER 22
CULTURE AND DYNAMICS

HERE'S THE TRUTH...

Culture is not a given. Like trust, culture can be destroyed in a split second.

IN SPEAKING OF PROGRESS, culture and the dynamics of a workplace can kill progress if they don't correlate. Combined, however, progress can be optimal. You can make all the progress in the world, but if you have a workplace culture that doesn't support the progress made, then progress won't last long.

Culture and workplace dynamics are big factors today, especially after the COVID-19 pandemic. Culture kind of took a back seat when everybody was let go of their jobs and when organizations transitioned over to remote working options. Although everyone was still working, remote offices changed the dynamic of the workplace, expanding it beyond the brick-and-mortar walls and into the employees' homes. It a matter of weeks, thousands of organizations had to make quick changes to how they operated based on survival. It forced the dynamics to change without any real notice.

Leadership and culture go hand in hand. In my experience, I've never had a great leader and a poor culture. Both were great, average, or poor. Your culture is a direct reflection of how you lead. However, in larger organizations that are broken down into smaller departments and sections, you could have a poor culture on the bigger scale, but a great culture and leader on the smaller scale.

I've had outstanding leaders at the highest levels who fostered great cultures to the smallest levels. And then again, I've also had poor leaders at the highest levels who seemed hell-bent on destroying good culture at the lowest levels.

> "Culture doesn't come from somewhere; it comes from someone."
>
> — Brian Knight

In this chapter, the focus is on how your leadership affects the culture around you and the bigger picture of culture. Your leadership plays a role in the larger culture of the organization. No matter where you are at in the food chain, your leadership plays up and down the chain. The top will see how you are doing, or should, and the people below will look up. How you lead will determine how they view you, and therefore, how they view your culture and dynamics.

Keep this in mind: Progress is also made because people want to work. They enjoy coming to work, or at least don't mind it, and can tolerate the workplace. If they don't, and the culture and dynamics don't fit them, progress will take a hit.

CULTURE

Culture can be expressed and defined so many ways, and rightfully so, because it's a very diverse subject. It is also another make-or-break principle of leadership. If you don't think culture matters that much, I challenge you to step inside an organization that prioritizes profits over people. Then step inside an organization that is people-centric. The answer will be simple. Culture is everything.

> "Corporate culture matters. How management chooses to read its people impacts everything for better or for worse."
>
> — Simon Sinek

What is culture to you? Take a second and think about it. What does it mean? What is its importance? What is your role?

Culture is an umbrella that encompasses things like language, religion, cuisine, social habits, music, and many other things. The customs, beliefs, and even attitudes all fall under the culture umbrella. We often think of culture as your background, where you are from, and how you were raised. That's very true and forms the basis for what culture is and can be. We all have different backgrounds and cultural upbringings that define who we are and even explain a little about us. And just like in life, we have a culture at home that we live in, and we have a culture at work that we live in. They two aren't the same, but they can have things in common.

We understand, or at least should understand, that a workplace isn't going to be like home. It won't be decorated the same, it won't have the same vibe, and the people won't be the same people that are at home. That's pretty self-explanatory, but organizations often forget that people don't leave their culture at home; they bring it with them. And just because they brought it with them doesn't mean it works well in the workplace.

The problem with culture is that we assume it's a given. We assume that the workplace comes with a culture, and that as a new leader we can just walk in and step right into the culture. We assume the cultural backgrounds of everyone on the team will mesh together and form the work culture, with little effort required. It's not true, and it's why leaders fail almost immediately ninety percent of the time—because they have assumptions about culture dynamics.

As a leader, you determine culture. Yes, many organizations and teams already have a culture and established dynamics. Some are highly functioning, and others need work. But leaders need to understand that they can make or break culture and change the dynamics by just showing up.

A workplace culture is a mesh of what everyone brings to the table. It's a mixture of many cultures and backgrounds all in one pot. Your job as a leader is to mix the pot well and bring everyone together. Together you all will determine what kind of culture the workplace has. Maintaining that culture is important, as when things get out of hand people will lose faith in the culture.

In the military we fostered a culture of zero tolerance. For certain unacceptable behaviors, there was no tolerance at all. Zero. These behaviors included sexual harassment and sexual assault. There was a zero-tolerance understanding and behaviors like this would not be allowed. Unfortunately, these behaviors happen, and it's disgusting. The culture of not allowing it is fine, and to be expected. I expected it out of every place I worked at. The problem the Air Force had was they said, "zero tolerance," but when someone high-ranking was accused of sexual harassment, they didn't maintain "zero tolerance." In fact, in order to keep the peace, they would just ask that person with rank to retire.

If it was truly zero tolerance, wouldn't they have shown them the door? People who are high in rank earned that rank through time, and even decades of work. So why give them a break? The result was, and still is, a culture of getting slapped on the hand for something you should see jail time for. I'm glad to see the shift changing in the DoD now, and serious consideration to trying sexual offenses in civilian courts as opposed to military courts. This would take the military bias out of it, and instead of saving careers we could eliminate the problem from our ranks. The only way to get to a true zero-tolerance policy is to have no tolerance for the offenses.

The entire problem with the issues above is failure to follow through. If you say something you need to mean it. Zero tolerance means zero tolerance. I don't care if you are a four-star general with almost forty years in service. If you broke the rules, after almost forty years you should have known better. Yes, you might lose your retirement, but after forty years of preaching zero tolerance and you still didn't understand it yourself, well, maybe you deserved it. I don't have a lot of sympathy for you. I do for the victims, and the people who have to pay for the failures of broken policy and the actions of others. We crush culture when policy only becomes words instead of mentality.

Examples like this are how people lose faith in workplace culture and leaders. If you have a culture of zero tolerance, when your best employee breaks the rules on a serious issue, you have to give them the boot. You have to follow through with the standards you have set to back up your developed culture and fire them. If you don't, the consequences are much larger.

It won't be easy to fire one of your top performers, but if you set the standard, you must follow through. The rest of your team is watching, waiting to see how you react. You want to keep that culture of zero tolerance? You've got to follow through on what you said. You've established the standards of behavior within your culture, and you must support them.

I believe that as a leader you should choose your words carefully. Talking tough will only make you look like a fool. You should have realistic standards that help define the workplace culture. Firing someone for showing up five minutes late is a bit drastic. However, firing someone over sexually harassing another coworker or stealing from the company makes a lot more sense. You can't have that behavior in your culture, as it is damaging to others who live in that culture.

As leaders, we must take decisive action on things that affect the culture. It's so incredibly important to how the team performs. A sour culture will only foster sour people, and vice versa.

CHAPTER 22

"Culture eats strategy for breakfast."

— *Peter Drucker*

DYNAMICS

Like culture, dynamics have a lot to do with people. You see a lot of dynamic workplaces now as society has embraced a more relaxed corporate mantra. You see large tech companies like Google, Apple, and Facebook allowing their employees to wear jeans to work. Suits and ties aren't dead, but they aren't nearly as popular as they used to be.

Now companies not only have more relaxed dress standards, but they are also embracing employee-centric strategies that encourage higher performance. Everything from four-day work weeks all the way to employee nap time (which I think is crazy, but something I'd like to see!). Organizations have become very dynamic parts of our society through the embracement of new norms.

Organizational dynamics stimulate growth, development, and even change within a system. Outstanding examples are dress code. Normally five days out of the week, people are expected to dress up. Some companies have even started requiring normal work attire four days out of the week, with Fridays designated as casual days. Jeans and comfortable shoes are encouraged so people can let their hair down and ease into the weekend. This little change to the workplace dynamics can change things for the better.

I also saw one company who did casual Mondays. The idea was to take the stress off of people who prepared for work on Sunday nights. Instead, jeans and other more casual clothing were encouraged on Monday so that people could just jump right into their week without feeling stuffy.

Being a dynamic leader means you are on the creative side of reality. You are open to new things, new ideas, and new ways of thinking. I've spoken to many leaders in the corporate world who didn't feel as if I was qualified to speak about leadership outside the military. Well, in fact, I'm quite qualified.

In the military we have a culture that is founded on standards and performance. We focus on the mission, getting the job done, and taking care of people. Without people we have no mission, and without a mission, we don't defend freedom. Sounds simple and not very dynamic, but just because it's simple and straightforward doesn't mean it isn't diverse in its execution.

Dynamic leaders exist in the military, as they exist in the corporate world. The difference is the military has different standards, and in many cases, higher standards. But that doesn't mean that we have boring dynamics. It just means the standards are set because there are higher stakes, more at risk. How we get the job done is a different topic.

Being a dynamic leader is to be creative, open, and flexible. It means you can react differently to individuals and situations. A dynamic leader is not one who is constrained by the rules, as they know the rules but understand the values.

I view dynamics in the workplace as something that is continually shifting. It's something that as a leader you must understand and be able to shift as well. I believe people in the military understand this better than anyone, as we move a lot. That means if I move away today, someone is replacing me tomorrow. The dynamics of the group I just left changed with my vacancy and changed again when my replacement was added. Same with the new organization I'm entering. The new organization changed when someone left and will change again when I'm added. Military commanders and senior leaders have to shift, as the dynamics and even culture change when adding or taking away new members.

Dynamics is important to understand when we talk about culture as it directly affects it. Leaders must also be dynamic in their leadership, as a one-size-fits-all approach likely won't work. Dynamic leaders can progressively clarify and refine their philosophies in order to suit the needs of the organization. That doesn't mean having to change their values or beliefs, but instead changing their approach to leading and holding those same values and standards.

"Life is the dynamic, creative edge of reality."

CHAPTER 23
FAILURE

HERE'S THE TRUTH...

Failure occurs more often than success.

LEADERS FAIL. They fail all the time. They sometimes fail when they didn't do anything at all. Sometimes that failure is because someone they lead failed, and therefore, they failed too. Leadership fails all the time.

There will be failure, lots and lots of failure, and that's perfectly fine. It will impede progress and frustrate you. It will destroy morale and motivation and make people cry. Failure sucks. It's never easy to deal with, especially when you are heavily invested in something. It's never easy and never will be. The day failure becomes easy to accept as a leader, you have failed yourself. It should be crushingly disappointing. Every. Single. Time.

> "Failure is not the opposite of success. It's part of success."
> — Arianna Huffington

However, you have to crawl before you can walk, and walk before you can run. I remember watching all of my kids learn to walk. It involved a ton of failures over the course of several weeks and months. More falling down than moving forward at first. And then it was more steps than falling down. Then it was hardly any falling down at all. But it took time to perfect that process, and yet, no matter how old you are, you are still at risk of falling down again. One would argue that the older you get, the risk of falling down begins to increase again, coming almost full circle. If you are me, you randomly have issues with your balance and fall over for no reason.

One of my wife's favorite stories is how I randomly fell down in the middle of a mall parking lot. No reason at all. I didn't trip over anything, nobody pushed me, shoelaces completely tied. I just took a wrong step and fell down. It was dramatic and sudden. My pride hurt worse than my physical pain did. It was embarrassing, and all I did was take a wrong step. That's how simple it was, and that's how simple failure can be. I wasn't trying to fail, but it happened anyway. I walk all the time, so you'd think I'd have that down by now! But no, I sure don't. And leading people is the exact same way. You rarely intend to fail or take the wrong steps, but it will happen anyway no matter how hard you try to prevent it.

The quicker you can understand that failure will happen, the quicker you can flourish as a leader. People who are afraid of failure spend more time running from it in an attempt to prevent it. Instead, embrace that failure might happen and use failures as an opportunity to grow. So many people get this all wrong and put their efforts toward NOT failing. That is a total waste of time. Failure is going to come whether you like it or not. Instead, put your efforts into positive things and obtaining small milestones of success. Just like working toward preventing failure, by focusing on successful milestones, we are also trying to prevent failure without directly focusing on it. The focus instead is on small goals and milestones, refocusing ourselves and the team on goal accomplishment instead of failure avoidance. The difference in mentality between the two paths is night and day. By focusing on preventing failure, you are actually focusing on failing, and are more likely to fail.

A perfect example of this is physical fitness. In my military career, I took a physical fitness test twice a year. I trained, despite hating to run, three-to-five times a week. I focused on the three components of the test: 1.5-mile run, one minute of push-ups, one minute of sit-ups, and of course, my weight since they measured your abdominal circumference. I'm not a runner, and I actually hate running. Never liked running for the sake of running. I respect those that do, especially long-distance runners, because running in my opinion is the most boring activity in the world. It can't keep my attention and I hate it. However, I was tested on it, so I had to train on it. And here are the facts: when I trained

CHAPTER 23

scared, I failed to achieve my ideal time on the 1.5-mile run. Almost every time. You know why? Because I was trying to avoid failure. My performance was throttled, limited in what it could do. I spent much needed energy on the wrong things.

I eventually put myself on a training regimen that instead focused on a whole-body fitness approach. Every day that I went to the gym I did forty-five minutes of cardio (treadmill, elliptical, rower, etc.), and an hour of weightlifting (finishing off the workout with one minute of push-ups and one minute of sit-ups). I stopped focusing on just the three components of the fitness test and started focusing on my entire body's fitness needs so I could be physically fit, not prepared for the fitness test. I was no longer focused on avoiding failure and instead was focused on being in shape. I rarely had problems with the test with this approach, as I was focused on small milestones (increasing my bench press weight, adding resistance to the elliptical, or my speed on the rowing machine). By doing this, I was avoiding failure by focusing on the milestones, rather than focusing on not failing. Make sense? It's a huge difference in mentality.

Of course we never *want* to fail, and even when we try to succeed, failure still happens. I tried to get this book published for over a year. You know how many literary agents told me no? Dozens. I never intended for rejection to happen, yet it did anyway. In a way, I expected it to, because I understand that not everyone would be interested in this book concept. Some of those agents provided me some feedback, and some didn't at all. The feedback I did get went immediately into the idea bank, and I analyzed how I could improve. *No* is not only a complete sentence, but also an opportunity for the first *yes*.

For example, it is extremely rare for a team in professional sports to have a perfect season. In the National Hockey League, the most games ever won is a tie between the 1995–1996 Detroit Redwings and the 2018–2019 Tampa Bay Lightning at sixty-two games. They both still lost thirteen and sixteen games, respectively. In the NBA, the record was 72–10 by the 1995–1996 Michael Jordan-led Chicago Bulls until the 2015–2016 Golden State Warriors went 73–9. Still, no perfection. They all still lost. The 1972 Miami Dolphins are the only team in the history of the National Football League to go undefeated, from game one all the way until the Super Bowl. Nobody else has ever done it again. A few have gotten close, but nobody has been able to seal the deal since 1972, and the NFL was founded in 1920 as the American Football League, making it over one hundred years old.

Even with athletes competing at the highest level in their sport, these teams with dynamic leaders, large budgets, and more support than most small armies still couldn't obtain perfection. Every single one of them lost at one point but losing also helped them win. The Warriors, Bulls, and Dolphins all won their respective championships. Only the Redwings were the ones to lose, and they didn't even make it to the Stanley Cup, further proving that even with the best record you can still not win it all. And also proving that despite your best efforts, failure is inevitable.

In order to make progress as a leader, you must understand failure. It's going to happen to you, your team, and your organization. It's never convenient and almost always strikes at the wrong time. However, the difference between good leaders and bad leaders is how they manage failure.

Failure can be two things:
1. a small bump in the road, or
2. the end of the world.

The question becomes... *how do you handle it?*

In my experience, when failure hits, the best approach is to take a deep breath, think for a minute, and analyze the situation. Never try to decide in the moment as those decisions, like I've stated previously, will be emotionally influenced.

Instead, take a few minutes at the very least and think about it. Decide with your brain first and your heart second. Nine times out of ten, if you follow this approach and use your brain first and your heart second, your brain is in sync with your heart already. My gut has never failed me when I took a second to think about things and make an informed and composed decision.

I have, however, had to apologize about my decisions when I led with my heart first and didn't take the time to think about it. Remember this: you aren't God or Jesus. Nothing you do or don't do is going to end the world, so stop making decisions that way.

Last, failure is going to happen to not only you, but to your team. Your staff will be hit with failure. They will either experience it or see it firsthand. How you as a leader react to your own failures, as well as theirs, will decide how they view you as a leader. Failure is not the end of the world, so don't react like it is. Instead, embrace failures as opportunities to learn, grow, and take a different look at the problem/situation. Failure is simply success in progress, and the greatest teacher if you let it teach you.

"Don't fear failure... in great attempts it is glorious even to fail."

— *Bruce Lee*

CHAPTER 24

LEADERSHIP IS NOT FOR SALE

HERE'S THE TRUTH...
You don't need to sell yourself to anyone.

LEADERSHIP IS NOT FOR SALE. It is not a product you sell to people, to your subordinates. You don't ask them to buy it and take it home to enjoy. It's not a TV, a microwave, or a new car. It's none of that. And if you have to sell yourself to people, you are doing it all wrong.

It should present your leadership in a manner that people want to listen, follow, and be guided by you. They shouldn't have to question it or consider it. Leadership should be influential while encouraging people to follow. I've made tons of purchases in my life, and I questioned and analyzed many of them. Many people do as well because spending money, even in small amounts, is an important investment. But I've also made other purchases that I didn't question, like buying my wife comfortable work shoes. She's on her feet all day. Comfortable shoes are a must. I rarely question it. Same goes with my work attire. I need to be comfortable, so I don't question the functionality of my work clothing, especially shoes and pants. I don't question any of these things because I understand their value and what they provide. These things are not for sale, because I need them in my life. I would pay much more money for good-functioning work shoes that I wear daily as opposed to regular tennis shoes that I maybe only wear on the weekends. As a leader, you are not for sale. You are not selling anything.

> "Leadership is action, not position."
>
> — Donald H. McGannon

People should invest in your leadership like a good pair of shoes for work. It's not optional; it's something they must have in their life. If you are trying to convince people to trust you or do what you say, you are for sale, and instead of a leader you are now a salesperson. Stop it. You need to reevaluate big time and consider those three questions at the beginning of the book.

1) WHAT DO YOU DO?

This one is simple. Do they know you by your title, by "the boss," or by your name? There is a difference. The difference lets you know how they view you and understand what you do. If you are "the boss," then they just see you as a decision maker. If they call you by your name, or even a nickname (we had call signs and nicknames on active duty), they understand you on a more personal level and are comfortable working with you. This generally means they understand your role in their life. You should be able to gauge if your followers and teammates understand what you do with this simple exercise. Evaluate it constantly.

2) WHAT CAN YOU DO TO MAKE THEIR LIFE BETTER? .

Sales professionals fail at converting because they offer nothing of value. Nothing they are offering appears to be making the audience's life any better. So it does not incline the audience to take interest or really listen. Are you providing something that can make their life better? As a leader, offer something that they know will make their work life easier, and therefore, their life at home easier because work doesn't suck. Or if work sucks, they understand the suck (Embrace the Suck, as we say in the military), and they know without a doubt that you are in the suck with them, waist deep, getting your hands dirty as well. Leaders should make things better, not worse.

3) HOW DO THEY BUY FROM YOU?

A great website doesn't sell you anything. It provides value in return for your time. E-commerce is huge, but it only takes up a small sliver of the internet. A great website convinces you on the first page to want

CHAPTER 24

more, getting you to buy into what they are offering. Yes, of course there are plenty of websites selling products. But that's not necessarily why you visited that site. You visited because you had a personal need or interest. Your curiosity piqued, and you had to check it out. There was value that you wanted more of.

In marketing, it's important to help the consumer decide to purchase something. If you want to sell more product and make more profit, you must sell the product before it's even exchanged for currency. The value needs to be there before anybody will even visit. Same with a website, and it's the exact same with leadership. We aren't selling anything, but we do want you to buy it.

So how do your followers buy from you? Are you selling instead of offering value? People want to invest in worthy things, not listen to sales pitches. Look at your approach and make some changes. Don't sell—instead, offer value. If you have to sell your leadership, you aren't doing leadership correctly.

A big turnoff to me is when you shop for a new vehicle and the salesperson at the dealership tries to talk you into something you don't want. They aren't concerned with your value, just their commission off the sale. Well, I don't need a brand-new minivan; I need a used truck. I know the minivan brand new is like $40K, but I need a used truck for around $25K. Or when I ask to see used models, you point me toward the new models for nearly fifty thousand more and explain that with the dealership financing you can get me in one of those today. I don't need that. I need value, not commission for your bank account.

I bring up the three questions above because it should have come full circle now. The algorithm you've built, or the one I've described that I use, should help to answer these three questions. If not, reevaluate. But in order to provide value as a leader, you must seek and understand value yourself. Leadership is a two-way street. Leading people and being led are the lanes. You, as odd as it sounds, must occupy both.

> *"Success is the sum of small efforts repeated day in and day out."*
>
> — *Robert Collier*

Great leaders understand that talking is cheap and actions rule all. I've said I in this book a lot while describing my concepts and philosophies, but in real leadership applications I forbid the use of the word I. I make massive attempts at never using it. You are a leader, but not when it only comes from you. The word I comes from a place of only self-inclusion and alienates people. It makes them feel as if the only important person in a conversation is the speaker, and nobody else. It makes them feel like you are talking to them, and that what you are saying doesn't apply to you. *I* is a toxic word when used frequently in the workplace. Want to rule the workplace? Get rid of the word I. Use we, and don't let it be a hollow word.

Remember back when I talked about being a self-licking ice cream cone? Here's why. Nobody rules the workplace. Nobody. And those that think they do are in for a rude awakening at some point. My way or the highway doesn't work anymore—those days are long gone. People today want to know we value them as members of the organization, and your greatest asset is treating them like it.

Does this mean rolling out the red carpet for them and giving away so many bonuses that you can no longer afford your own salary? Nope, not at all. But it means showing more appreciation than just a paycheck.

Ruling the workplace can mean two things, depending upon how you read it. It can mean ruling, like a king, with an iron fist, and expecting people to bow before you. Think, *"Game of Thrones"* with the Iron Throne, bending the knee, and the Starbucks cup left on the table.

Or...

Ruling the workplace can mean you are in full control, the puppet master, the card dealer, the genius behind the scenes watching the plot play out. Think of it like a mad scientist, the guy who put all these things together to create a wonderful masterpiece designed to take over. In essence, you are locked into the culture, vibe, and understanding of the organization and its members so well that the machine runs itself. You've tapped into the neurological side of the organization and fully understand it. You rule over it because you are so in tune with it that you simply give it what it needs, and it runs itself.

Nobody rules over us. We are all citizens of this great nation, not subjects that need to be ruled. Same goes for leadership in the workplace. Nobody is a ruler. There is no king, no chief, no dictator. The people you follow are not subjects needing to be ruled, and you are no king (or queen). You are a leader who can have a greater impact.

So what do I mean by "rule the workplace"? I simply mean you are a rock star, with people who are rock stars, and you have a lot of success. You and the team and just rocking it. But not because the big deals are coming in, sales are up, or big advancements have occurred. You are rocking it because every aspect of the organization is running like a well-oiled machine. A machine that you've fine-tuned over time because you've paid close attention to the little things. All is good and all is well because you have dedicated the time to making the entire operation great, not just the things that are important to you. You want to be the talk of the organization, the place people desire to work in. All eyes are on you and your team, as you guys have got it figured out.

To truly rule the workplace, it's about servant leadership and serving others. Full self-awareness and ability to be humble, vulnerable, an expert at times, and lost in others. It's about empowerment, knowledge, and the ability to see all sides of people, processes, and the truth. Leadership sucks. It's hard work, and it's not for everybody. A lot of leaders have it backwards and they worry only about what might make them look good or bad and cannot focus on the big picture. But in reality, that big picture can actually make them look good long-term instead of short-term. Real leadership is about everything BUT you.

Last, let me leave you with this. People can see through the bullshit, so don't bullshit them. It's maybe the single most important tip I can offer, and honestly the one tip I default to all the time. Don't bullshit your team, your people, or the people who work around you. Shoot it to them straight, in a respectful and honest matter, and leave no doubt. Treat them as experts until they prove otherwise, and then invest in them to make them experts again. Full, transparent, and honest leadership. That level of honesty will create a level of trust that you can never build deliberately. Give them facts, give them real answers, or don't give them anything at all. It's better to say, "I don't know," than say, "Here's a bunch of bullshit."

Write those three questions down along with the algorithm you've developed (or use mine, either way), and post it in your office. Make sure not only that you can see it, but others can as well. Never shy away from talking about it or answering if someone asks about it. Leadership is to be shared. Leadership is a gift. Leadership is not for sale.

> "Leadership is a gift. It's given by those who follow.
> You have to be worthy of it."
> — 20th United States Air Force Chief of Staff

CHAPTER 25
FINAL MESSAGE

Below are the reasons I'm better than you:

1…
2…
3…

I'M NOT. The list is empty because there is no sense in trying to justify it. I'm just a normal guy who took everything into perspective and loves to talk leadership. You can too, and you should. Never value yourself over others and remember—the key to leadership is not just leading others, but also leading yourself. You are a constant work in progress.

Someone I follow on Instagram inspired the list above. She's a veteran, and her account is @themillenialveteran. I love her content, and love following her account. I suggest you do too. She posted that same list above, with a message that followed that really made me think. I asked her if I could reference it in my book because I thought it was so impactful.

The message was simple. The reason the space after the numbers is blank is because there really isn't anything that makes me better than you. In fact, you might even be better than me. But in reality, we are all good at some things and bad at others. Hell, we might even complement each other. Complete strangers working together, using their strengths to supplement each other's weaknesses. Isn't that a crazy thought? Well, it shouldn't be a crazy thought, because that's exactly how things should work.

The rest of that message is as follows...

Success has nothing to do with skill, effort, or accomplishments. Rather, it has everything to do with perspective. Defining your success is relative and must be humble. What is success to you?

To answer her call to action... For me, success is reaching people, helping them grow, and watching them succeed. Many people are afraid of this approach as they feel they might create competition. Yes you are, but in another sense, you are creating an extension of you. If you've done it right, you've infused them with some of your teachings, influence, or positivity. You might not be able to take credit, but you can obtain self-fulfillment by watching them rise, knowing you had a part in it. Now they will go on as a version of you, learning to discover themselves. People will feed off of them, repeating the process. We grow leaders by being great leaders ourselves. It's all about perspective.

I've obtained success and even been rewarded for it. I've won large awards before, and you know who was responsible for them? My team. I couldn't have reached that level of success without having a great team. Yes, I was their leader, and worked very hard myself, but if they didn't follow me, then what kind of leader would I have been? I'd just be a hard worker dictating other people do the same. Leadership is about perspective.

During that time, I found a balance of me leading them in the areas they needed to be led, adjusting my priorities to fit theirs, and finding common ground. I empowered them through my leadership, and they did remarkable things. The tools they needed to thrive were provided, and I got out of the way. I nudged now and then, high-fived when necessary, and provided my thoughts as required. The rest they did themselves. It sounds simple, but it was an orchestrated effort over a long period of time.

> "When a leader embraces their responsibility to care for people instead of caring for numbers, then people will follow, solve problems, and see to it that the leader's vision comes to life right away."
>
> — Simon Sinek

I was fortunate to take the credit because I was in charge. And when I won that award, I told everyone who congratulated me I was thankful for them, as I simply represented their hard work and dedication. Those impressive accomplishments were already inside of them, just waiting to break out. They needed the right push of motivation and confidence to get moving. A skilled leader can discover this and provide what is necessary for people to achieve it. Prominent leaders don't stand above all on a platform and point, direct, and dictate. They evaluate, analyze, and then take action. Ego-less action. A humble and honest perspective. Never forcing the square peg into the round hole.

I could go on and on about leadership and what you need to do, but what you need to do is find your way. Use what you've read here, what you need, and what you hear from others and build yourself. Never stop building yourself and never stop growing. Empower others and be a leader, not a boss. Great leaders don't have to work that hard at influencing people. A boss has to work at it, often declaring their status and making it widely known. They are salespeople just hoping to convince people that what they are saying is real and true. But leadership isn't for sale. Besides, if you have to sell yourself to others, then you haven't done a very good job of selling in the first place.

I hope by now you have a good idea of what your leadership algorithm might look like, or how you would implement the one talked about in this book. As I've stated previously, leadership is the simplest, most complex, and difficult thing in the world. The approach can be easy and simple, the execution difficult and frustrating. However, I've found that having a purpose, fueled by a process and a strategy, can at least get you started off on the right foot.

There is a lot of pressure on leaders to get things done and do them well. We expect them to lead people unconditionally and basically read minds. It's a hard thing to do, something nobody ever really masters. I've met tons of skilled leaders and the best ones all said that they were still figuring it all out. Leadership is a challenging road to travel, but instead of focusing on the challenge, work on focusing on the solution.

I struggled to close out this book, as I wanted to leave every reader feeling at least inspired and/or motivated. As quotes have been a recurring theme, I think it would be appropriate to leave you with one of my favorites from Simon Sinek:

> "If your actions inspire others to dream more, learn more, do more and become more, you are a leader."

And that's the truth. You've heard it.

ACKNOWLEDGMENTS

HERE'S THE LAST TRUTH...

Once I stopped thinking I had something to prove to myself, and instead something to offer to everyone, providing it became a lot easier.

I have no problem talking about leadership, business, or my military experiences, so I thought writing a book would be easy. I was wrong. Writing a book is much harder than I thought. I'm grateful to Chris Schafer and Tactical 16 for seeing my vision, understanding the purpose, and being patient. Writing should be therapeutic, especially for veterans, and Tactical 16 sees it that way. I never once received an email or phone call asking when I'd submit or be ready to publish. It was a check-in. *How are you doing? How's the writing going? What date did you have in mind to release?* They provided the publishing expertise, and I provided the content. Together we hit a home run I believe. And when I was ready to submit, they were ready to roll.

I'd like to thank all my past coworkers, supervisors, and people I've interacted with. I've had some great experiences and some horrible ones, but I've taken something from all of it.

I'd like to thank my mother, stepdad, and my father for raising me up. We've had some ups and some downs, and because of you all I strove to be better. I reached for the stars and pushed hard. I made mistakes; I got back up, and you guys never wavered. I know at times it was tough to watch, but I appreciate the fact that you knew when to step in and when to leave me alone. I learned valuable lessons that can't be quantified or described with a dollar value. You saw potential in me that it took forever for me to see, but I'm so thankful that you never lost that vision. I hope I've done you proud. You never quit on me, and I'll never forget that.

To my kids—I love you guys. I don't say it enough. I'm proud of all of you, and I probably don't say that enough. What you've given me over the years has been a blessing, and I'm forever thankful. You've taught me more than I ever could imagine, and I'm a different and better person today because of you. Words can't express it. Go be better than I was. Reach for the stars and don't let anyone ever tell you that you can't do something. When I graduated from high school, I never thought in a million years I'd join the military, let alone write a book. I not only accomplished both of those, but I have many awards, letters, and other items that have recognized my superior performance. I let life guide me, and I am truly one of the top people in my field and it's been because I took nothing for granted and I always worked hard, harder than the next guy. Don't grow up and be me, be you, be better and know I'll always be proud of you for sticking to that.

To my wife, my rock, my heart, my teammate. Thank you. Thank you for never quitting on me. Thanks for seeing what my parents saw in me, and even more, and never letting me settle. I wanted to throw in the towel many times, on many endeavors, and you never allowed me to. When I was up against a wall, you had my back. Thanks for always telling me, despite my crazy ideas, that they were always good. Thanks for never telling me I was stupid, or something I wanted was stupid. Thanks for always being supportive while also keeping me grounded and attached to reality. Thanks for making me a dad, the greatest job in the world. You will never know how much it all meant. I don't know what I'd do without you.

To my mentors, influencers, and inspirations. Thank you. I can't name you all, as so many people have inspired me over the years. If I thank anybody by name, I'll thank the veteran community for always being authentic and supportive. When I need help I look toward another veteran, as nobody takes care of you better than a fellow brother or sister.

To Shane Schmitt, Johnny Lupo, and Jason Ware. Thank you from the bottom of my heart for seeing something in me that no other leaders could. Thanks for giving me a chance, thanks for supporting me to reach higher, and most importantly, thanks for being great friends. And of course, thanks for letting me be a part of the process. I learned more than you can imagine, and my growth made me stronger. I owe you guys. Beers are on me next time we see each other.

To Chief Master Sergeant (Retired) John Gebhardt, my first chief. Thank you for those initial lessons as a young airman. They stuck with me forever, and I never forgot where I came from. You ensured I started off on the right path, and I made sure to pay that forward every day for twelve years, and then continued it once I was out. I still remember our conversations, as they are some of the best conversations of my military career. You did what was right, when it needed to be done. You taught me authenticity and honesty, and I won't forget it.

To my family, friends, and teammates on social media, especially LinkedIn… thank you. Your support has always been outstanding, from my awful first videos to having me on your live streams and recorded YouTube shows, as well as podcasts and other forms of media. I appreciate the chats, the support, and the fellowship. Too many to name; but thank you all.

To my coach Tracy Borreson, who helped me find my voice. I didn't believe I needed a coach until I met Tracy. After much thinking and getting my ego out of the room, I hired Tracy to help me find my voice. I quickly realized I couldn't put all this knowledge in my head together alone, and Tracy navigated me through the lengthy process of finding my voice as a brand and helped establish what you see today. You don't know how much that meant to me, as it gave me the motivation and confidence to jump into endeavors I would normally not have. If you need to find your voice, your brand, and expand your business, find Tracy Borreson on LinkedIn and give her a shout!

Lastly, thanks to everyone for the support. I'm sure I forgot about somebody, but it's not because I'm not thinking about you. Writing the acknowledgments was the hardest part of this book. Thanks for reading. I only hope that the words I've put into these pages help at least one person, and then they turn around and help another. From there the fire will rise.

— Jeff

ABOUT THE AUTHOR
JEFF CLARK

Author Jeff Clark is a 12-year veteran of the US Air Force with years of leadership experience. His wife Shannon is a dermatology physician, and he is dad to four kids (Kyler, Hayden, Austin, and Maddie). Jeff grew up in Enid, Oklahoma, a small but growing town in the northwest part of the state. He spent much of his childhood outdoors—fishing, hunting, playing baseball, and helping out on family friends' farms.

During his Air Force career, Jeff directly supported Operations Enduring Freedom and Iraqi Freedom, gathering over 4 years of experience in joint command environments. While serving, Jeff also obtained two undergraduate degrees, a graduate degree, and three certifications (Lean Six Sigma, Technical Training, and Executive Leadership).

In 2017 Jeff was medically retired from active duty, and in early 2018 he returned to service again—this time as a government civilian. Throughout his government career he has held multiple leadership positions at various levels, and in 2019 he was recognized as the Major Command and HQ Air Force Civilian Supervisor of the Year. His expertise in leading others has evolved into multiple executive publications and a successful private leadership coaching business, all the while increasing his desire to share his "leadership algorithm" concept with others.

Currently, Jeff hosts a podcast called "Course of Action" and donates his time volunteering with multiple veteran service organizations while watching his kids grow up. He is also currently working towards his doctorate in Business Administration and Strategy.

ABOUT THE PUBLISHER
TACTICAL 16

Tactical 16 Publishing is an unconventional publisher that understands the therapeutic value inherent in writing. We help veterans, first responders, and their families and friends to tell their stories using their words.

We are on a mission to capture the history of America's heroes: stories about sacrifices during chaos, humor amid tragedy, and victories learned from experiences not readily recreated — real stories from real people.

Tactical 16 has published books in leadership, business, fiction, and children's genres. We produce all types of works, from self-help to memoirs that preserve unique stories not yet told.

You don't have to be a polished author to join our ranks. If you can write with passion and be unapologetic, we want to talk. Go to Tactical16.com to contact us and to learn more.

CPSIA information can be obtained
at www.ICGtesting.com
Printed in the USA
BVHW051319190522
637461BV00005B/15